Decorating with
Needlepoint

Joan Scobey and Marjorie Sablow

CHL CREATIVE HOME LIBRARY®
In Association with **Better Homes and Gardens**®
Meredith Corporation

Photography by John Garetti, New York City

⌂ CREATIVE HOME LIBRARY®

©Meredith Corporation, 1975. All rights reserved
First edition. Second printing, 1976
Printed in the United States of America

Library of Congress Catalog Card Number: 75-18983
SBN: 696-34600-1

About the Authors

For many years *Joan Scobey* has acted on her concern with the quality of life for women, particularly those whose lives revolve primarily around the home. From her first book, *Creative Careers for Women* (co-authored), which suggested how women could work part-time at home, to her many subsequent crafts books, she has written about the substantial satisfactions available to women when they add a creative dimension to their lives.

Ms. Scobey's books about needlecraft (some of them co-authored) include *Rugs and Wall Hangings*, *Do-It-All-Yourself Needlepoint*, *Needlepoint from Start to Finish*, *Rugmaking from Start to Finish*, all illustrated by Marjorie Sablow, and *Celebrity Needlepoint*. She also co-authored *Gifts from the Kitchen* and *Gifts from your Garden*, as well as an appealing series of children's reactions to and observations about home life.

After graduating from Smith College, Ms. Scobey studied in France and contributed travel articles to the *European Herald Tribune*. She has served as the writer and producer of a children's radio program and as a free-lance editor for an art foundation, an encyclopedia, and her local school board. She has also been assistant editor of a trade magazine and has written many articles of general interest to women for most of the popular women's magazines.

A native New Yorker, today Ms. Scobey lives outside New York with her husband and two sons and is active in the civic and political life of her town.

An experienced commercial artist, *Marjorie Sablow* has designed dinnerware patterns and Christmas cards in addition to her needlework creations, which are used by several national craft kit manufacturers and well-known New York City specialty shops. Marjorie devised the designs for and illustrated four books on soft crafts with Joan Scobey; she has also illustrated a book on jewelry making.

Interest in art pervades Ms. Sablow's life—she has a degree in fine arts from Cornell University and studied commercial art at the Traphagen School of Design. Hand painting pillows and making freestanding acrylic art objects are also a part of her professional pursuits. During her leisure time, Ms. Sablow visits museums and galleries to keep up with innovations in the art world, advises friends on interior decorating, designs stage sets, and does make-up for theatrical performances.

Ms. Sablow, her husband, and two children live in New Rochelle, New York.

To Lilybird

and to so many others whose hands enriched this book and who, in the doing, came to know the pleasures of decorating with needlepoint—Shelley Akabas, Doris Brown, Judy Coulter, Hilde Fuchs, Betty Fuld, Joan Gevertz, Harriet and Victor Goldberg, Renee Herzog, Bobsy Hessberg, Corinne Katz, Barbara Kellman, Erna Lewine, Joanne Matthews, Lois Miller, Toni Miner, Fran Myers, Norma Myers, Alix Prince, Lenore Rosenbaum, Deena Rosenthal, Eugene Sablow, Barbara Sablow, Marilyn Schoenberger, Fred Soderquist, Esther Shay, Ann Spindel, Arlyne Steiner, Mimi Stillman, Nicki Tanner, Lucette Tarbox, Lillian Tucker, Janet Wells, and Ruth Wile.

No less are we indebted to Jane Wilson for her patience and wisdom as always.

We also want to thank Boussac of France, whose authorization of the use of the pattern "Villandry" in this book should not be considered an authorization to reproduce this pattern elsewhere.

Registered trademarks that appear in this book are: Velcro, Lucite, Plexiglas, Mylar, Scotchgard, Sharpie, Sobo, Elmer's Glue-All, Amco White Glue, Black Magic Tough Glue, and Dacron.

Contents

Introduction

Decorating with needlepoint is the joyous experience of creating things of beauty for that most personal of all environments—your home. Bringing warmth and design and texture, needlepoint furnishings are a unique contribution to family life, transcending by far their purely decorative values. And, as is true of many articles that are crafted—needlepoint has a longevity seldom matched by machine-made fabrics, enabling it to provide pleasure for succeeding generations.

Beyond its creative and heirloom qualities, needlepoint is an exciting decorating instrument. First, of course, it is a splendid heavy-duty upholstery fabric. And, because it is custom-made in every sense, it can extend the harmonious notes of your present color scheme or it can provide an unexpected and invigorating accent.

Because needlepoint should be closely related to other home furnishings, you will find that many of the designs in this book are derived from, and used with, other decorating fabrics—upholstery, carpeting, drapery. Utilize these designs as they fit into your home, freely substituting your own color schemes.

Happily, every room can use the warming touch of needlepoint—even the unlikeliest places.

You can brighten a kitchen with a bulletin board, breakfast stool pads, a telephone book cover, bookends to embrace the chef's cache of cook books. You can perk up a bathroom with trim on the window shade, a hanger for guest towels, a colorful can cover to hide unsightly toiletry containers. Your more public rooms are obvious showcases for needlepoint. This is especially true of the dining area, where frame chairs and a wood or glass table invite the warmth of needlepoint in the form of upholstered seats, tie-on pads, table runners, and napkin rings, window valances, and drapery tiebacks.

As your opportunities for needlepoint increase, guard against the temptation to overuse it. Displayed sparingly, each piece becomes more valued and special. Place a group of interrelated pillows on a sofa or a piano bench pad or an upholstered parson's table or a splendid rug—but don't put all of them together in the same room. Be especially wary of overburdening the living room with needlepoint; its upholstered furniture and focus of activity fairly entice an overabundance of stitchery. And always, above all, relate all your designs to the decor of your home, in terms of color, fabric, and scale.

How to Use the Book

As you can see from the table of contents, there are three major sections in the book; they are all interrelated. Section I. "Tools and Techniques," presents all the information needed—from cutting through working designs to all the finishing procedures required for the projects in Section II as well as practically every kind of decorating project.

All the decorative projects are in Section II, "Needlepoint for the Home." Each one is presented in a uniform format that clearly sets forth the specific instructions you will need. You will also be taught how to adapt designs to projects that have different dimensions. Last, but not least, a "Decorating Bonus" will suggest additional opportunities for decorating with needlepoint.

Section III, "Swatchbook of Needlepoint Designs," presents a number of allover repeat patterns that can be used with any of the projects in Section II. These swatches, taken together with the project designs in Section II, encompass a diversity of styles—a variety of Orientals, such as

Persian, Chinese, Japanese, Turkoman, contemporary abstracts, geometrics, a profusion of florals, and animals.

To make the best use of the book and increase its flexibility, don't be constrained by the limits of each project. You can, of course, make each article as set forth, stitching the suggested design on its designated project. But you can also use many of the designs and procedures interchangeably. For example, borrow the herbs from the bookends and plant them around the ice bucket, or adapt the folk art window shade trim for luggage-rack straps; use the tie-on tassels from the child's chair to trim a wall hanging, or the cording from a pillow to finish a mirror frame; use letters on the typewriter cover to personalize accessories.

Mix and match as you go, picking a favorite design from one project and an appealing technique from another, and then mating them with a third. Then, if you like, substitute your own color scheme so that the resulting furnishing is truly your own—not only done in your own fine hand, but displaying your own signature.

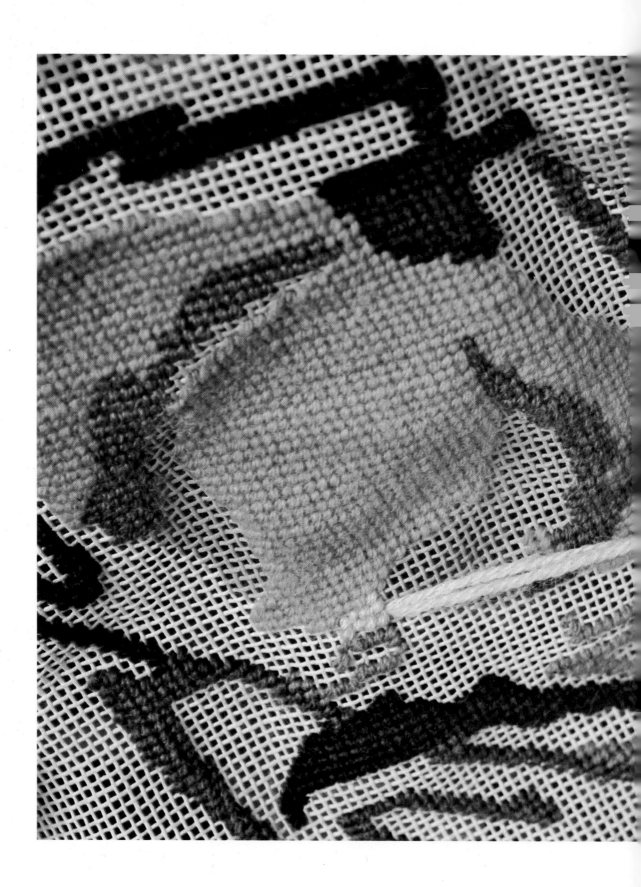

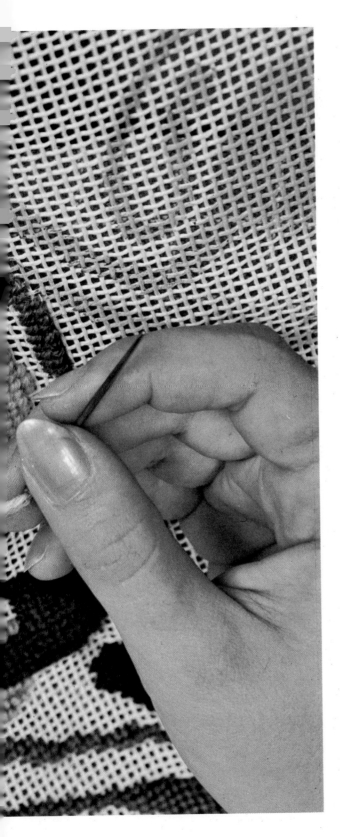

Basic Tools and Techniques

Their appealing textures and the glorious abundance of colors, shades, and tints that are available make needlepoint yarns enticing tools for decorating your home. The tools and techniques required to transform yarn and canvas into delightful home furnishings are presented in this section. First, a basic primer on the tools —canvas, needles, and yarns—will provide you with background information. Then comes a guide to the techniques, which covers everything from preparing canvas to the various techniques of finishing and assembling projects. Also included are directions for six stitches, plus helpful tips on blocking and stitching.

Read this section before beginning your projects. It will help you turn out professional-looking home furnishings of your own.

Tools

There are relatively few supplies needed for the needlepoint decorating projects in this book. You probably have most of them at home already. In addition to canvas, needles, and yarn, which are described in detail below, you will need the following:
• pair of small, pointed scissors for cutting yarn
• pair of large scissors for cutting canvas
• roll of 1-inch-wide masking tape for binding cut canvas edges
• sheet of brown wrapping paper or any large piece of paper for outlining projects
• indelible marker for tracing designs onto canvas
• white resin glue, such as Elmer's Glue-All, Slomon's Sobo Glue, Amco White Glue, for gluing canvas and bonding finished needlepoint to porous materials
• wooden or composition board for blocking canvas
• stainless steel T-pins for blocking canvas
• assorted sewing needles and threads for finishing projects

For some projects, special supplies are required. These are listed with the project under "Additional Materials."

Canvas

Needlepoint canvas is a coarsely woven grid, usually made of cotton, on which the horizontal and vertical threads are evenly spaced. The canvas has been stiffened with sizing to make stitching easier.

Canvas sizes are identified by the spacing of the threads—that is, by the number of threads contained per inch in one direction. For example, No. 10 canvas has ten threads to the inch and 100 intersections to the square inch; No. 12 canvas has twelve threads to the inch and 144 intersections to the square inch.

There are three principle types of canvas, differentiated by their weave:

Mono canvas. In mono canvas, single threads are woven to form the grid (see Figure 1). Mono canvas is easy and pleasant

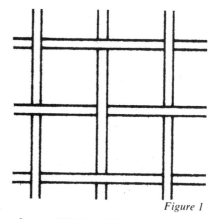

Figure 1

to work on. While stiff enough to hold the stitches, it becomes more flexible as you work and is nicely pliant by the time you are ready to mount it. Because the canvas is usually white, it takes a painted design well. However, certain stitches are not securely anchored on the single-thread intersections.

Penelope canvas. In penelope canvas, double threads are woven to form the grid (see Figure 2). You can work practically any

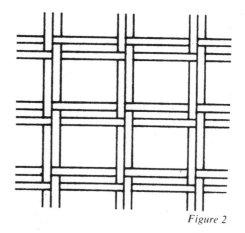

Figure 2

stitch on penelope, stitching over each double-thread intersection as if it were single. One appealing feature of penelope is that the double-thread intersections can be divided into four smaller intersections by spreading apart the canvas threads (see

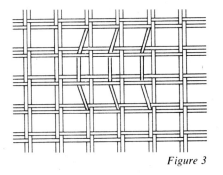

Figure 3

Figure 3). In this way, you can combine areas of fine detail and backgrounds of larger stitching on the same canvas. See the lamp base project on page 146 for examples of how this looks.

If you are not taking advantage of the split-intersection feature of penelope canvas, you may prefer to use mono canvas. The double threads of penelope make the jobs of counting and stitching intersections harder; also, the best penelope canvas is beige or ecru, and these don't provide as good a field for painted designs as white does. Joining canvas, too, is more difficult with penelope.

Interlocking canvas. In interlocking canvas, two vertical threads are woven around one horizontal thread to form the grid (see

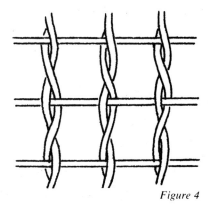

Figure 4

Figure 4). In an attempt to combine some advantages of mono and penelope in one canvas, interlocking canvas anchors stitches like penelope and forms clearly defined intersections like mono. It is excellent for any stitch and is particularly well suited for bargello. However, the rigid, interlocking weave is harsh on yarn, stiff to the touch, and makes it difficult to finish projects that require hemming, such as pillows. On the other hand, the interlocking weave allows you to cut close to the stitched needlepoint without fear of raveling the canvas threads— an advantage in many projects where you want to eliminate the bulk of a hemmed edge. This is a particularly attractive asset in such accessories as luggage-rack straps whose narrow widths don't easily allow for a hem.

Since the cut edges of interlocking canvas are finished with an overcasting stitch (see page 22), choose designs that can be bound in the color of the background or in a contrasting color; allover multi-patterns are hard to finish properly on the edges.

While all three types of canvas come in a variety of sizes, the most useful for home decorating projects are No. 10 and No. 12. They can be stitched fairly quickly and can reproduce a reasonable degree of design detail. For finer work on a small piece, you may want to use No. 14 canvas; any mesh smaller than No. 14, however, makes a decorating project tedious. For large items, you may want to consider No. 7 or No. 5 canvas for speed, but you will have to sacrifice some of the detail in the design. For each of the projects in Section II, the designated canvas is most appropriate for the particular design and required method of finishing.

Needles

Tapestry needles, which have blunt points and large eyes, are used for needlepoint. It is important that the needle pass comfortably through the canvas mesh and that the yarn slide easily through the eye to minimize abrasion. No. 18 and No. 19 needles are suitable for most of the projects in the book. For other projects, refer to the following guide:

CANVAS–NEEDLE GUIDE

Canvas size	Needle size
No. 5	No. 13
No. 7	No. 15
No. 8	No. 15
No. 10	No. 17, No. 18, No. 19
No. 12	No. 17, No. 18, No. 19
No. 14	No. 20
No. 16	No. 22

Yarns

Needlepoint yarn should be of excellent quality, especially when used for home furnishing projects that require durability. This means, first of all, that it should be made of wool with long, smooth fibers. It should also be mothproof and colorfast. Several kinds of yarn meet these specifications, including tapestry wool and crewel wool. The most versatile of them all, however is Persian wool.

Persian wool. This is a 2-ply wool that is loosely twisted into threads of three strands (see Figure 5). The strands can be separated

Figure 5

or can be used together as one thread. It is sold by many companies, but because the one distributed by Paternayan Bros., Inc. is widely available and comes in well over 300 shades, it is used in this book as the basis of all yarn estimates.

Persian wool is usually sold by the ounce, but you can sometimes buy it by the skein, by the half-ounce, or even by the thread.

Tapestry wool. Tapestry wool is widely available in a range of over fifty colors in most brands and comes in 40- or 100-yard skeins in matched dye lots. It is a 4-ply wool

that cannot be split for use with fine mesh canvas; it can, however, be doubled for use with coarse canvas.

Crewel wool. Crewel wool is a 2-ply wool that is sold in a variety of colors in 20- to 25-yard skeins. It is intended for use with finer-mesh canvas than is appropriate for the projects in this book.

Rug wool. Rug wool is excellent in quality and is recommended for projects using coarser-mesh canvas.

Knitting worsted. Although made of wool, knitting worsted has shorter fibers and is, therefore, less durable. It is not recommended for anything but wall hangings. For purely decorative purposes, many other less durable materials, such as silks, metallic threads, cotton embroidery, and various synthetic fibers can be used for wall hangings.

Estimating Amounts of Yarn

The yarn estimates given for each project are necessarily imprecise because they depend on so many variables—the tightness or looseness of individual work, the accuracy of the canvas count, and the fullness and, therefore, coverage of each strand, which is often affected by the yarn dye. These estimates are based on Paternayan Persian wool and will vary with other Persian yarns.

The most reliable estimate is one made by yourself. Before ordering yarn in quantity, stitch one length of the yarn you will use in the margin of your intended canvas. Count the number of stitches or measure the area covered by the test strand, and then calculate your total needs based on this figure.

If you want to estimate yarn for a project of your own dimensions, here are some miscellaneous guidelines arrived at by trial and error:

- A good working length of Persian yarn is about 32 inches. You get it by cutting a skein twice (once at each end).
- One length of Persian yarn makes about 85 stitches on No. 10 canvas, about 95 stitches on No. 12 canvas, and about 102 stitches on No. 14 canvas.
- To get a general yarn estimate, measure the area of the canvas in square inches and

then, for No. 10 canvas, divide that number by 4 and multiply by 6; for No. 12 canvas, divide that number by 4 and multiply by 5; on No. 14 canvas, divide that number by 3 and multiply by 4½.

In every case, your answer will be in number of threads, which must be translated into ounces. For Paternayan Persian, about forty-five 32-inch threads weigh one ounce.

• Try to buy sufficient yarn at the start, since dye lots sometimes vary in color. This is especially important for the background color, where even the slightest difference in dye lot can show. Slight variations of color are not as critical when the areas to be stitched are widely separated, but are jarring when the areas are contiguous.

• When making your yarn estimates, don't forget to take into account the number of strands you will be using—the full three-strand thread or just one or two strands.

The number of strands needed will vary according to type of yarn, stitch, and canvas. Use the following chart as a guide:

Yarn and Number of Strands per Stitch and Canvas Size				
Stitch	**No. 12**	**No. 10**	**No. 10 penelope (split)**	**No. 5**
Basketweave	Persian, 2 or 3 tapestry	Persian, 3 tapestry	Persian, 1	Persian, 8 or 9 tapestry, tripled rug
Continental	Persian, 2 or 3 tapestry	Persian, 3 tapestry	Persian, 1	Persian, 8 or 9 tapestry, tripled rug
Half Cross	Persian, 2 or 3 tapestry	Persian, 3 tapestry	not recommended	Persian, 8 or 9 tapestry, tripled rug
Scotch	Persian, 2 or 3 tapestry	Persian, 3 tapestry	not recommended	tapestry, tripled rug
Gobelin	Persian, 3 tapestry	Persian, 4	not recommended	rug
Brick	Persian, 3 tapestry	Persian, 4	not recommended	rug
Overcasting	Persian, 3 tapestry	Persian, 4	not recommended	rug

Techniques

Now that all the needed tools are at hand, here are the techniques that will enable you to transform them into delightful needlepoint projects for the home. The following instructions will show you how to handle the canvas, work the designs, and finish the projects.

Preparing Canvas

Although preparing a canvas for work involves little more than cutting the mesh and taping the edges, there are a few simple rules to remember:
• Cut the canvas at least 2 inches larger all around than the proposed needlepoint.
• Always cut the canvas in a rectangle (or square), even if you are planning a circular, triangular, or odd-shaped design. You will need the four opposing sides for blocking.
• Bind all cut edges of canvas with masking tape that is at least 1 inch wide. Narrower tape has a tendency to come loose.
• Lay the taped canvas on a piece of brown wrapping paper (or on a large sheet of any other kind of paper). Outline the canvas—not the actual design area—and make register marks at the corners and the center of each side. Marks should extend from the tape to the paper (see Figure 6). Lay the paper aside until you are ready to block your finished needlepoint.
• Plan your canvas layout with the selvage running up and down. Whenever you cut pieces of canvas, tape all edges and note the direction of the selvage. On penelope canvas, the closely paired threads usually run up and down, parallel to the selvage.
• When you use more than one piece of canvas for the same project, be sure that all selvages run in the same direction. You will find that although canvas mesh looks square, it really is not quite even, and that this discrepancy increases with the size of the canvas. Take particular care when making a

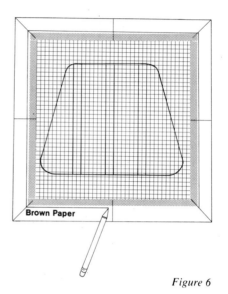

Brown Paper

Figure 6

matched set or when two pieces of canvas are to be joined.
• You can conserve canvas by laying out more than one design per canvas. Be sure to leave at least 3 inches between designs for finishing.
• Find the center of the canvas by folding the canvas in half lengthwise and then in quarters. This center point will be helpful in tracing the design onto canvas.

Making Custom Patterns

Some of the projects in this book will be made to your own dimensions, particularly the chairs, benches, and stools. Accurate measurements are essential. Wherever you can, use a steel or wooden rule. If using a fabric tape measure on upholstered pieces, check it first against a rigid rule to be sure it hasn't stretched.

For every project that must fit accurately, make a custom pattern and mark all pertinent dimensions on it. For flat and cylindrical objects, such as tabletops and ice buckets, you can make a pattern out of heavy brown wrapping paper (see Figure 7); for upholstered pieces, make the pattern out of muslin. If you are planning to replace padding, allow for new stuffing, which may be fuller than existing padding (see Figure 8).

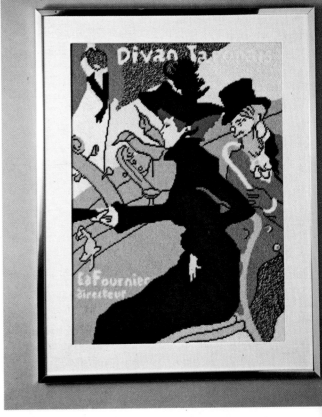

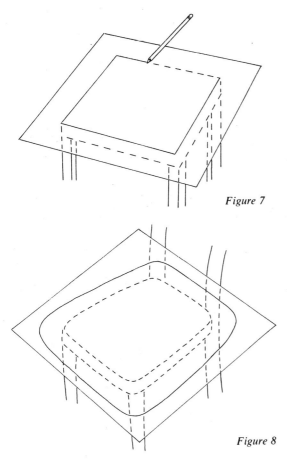

Figure 7

Figure 8

Mark all dimensions for the finished project; any additional requirements for seam allowance or finishing will be given with each particular project.

Copying Designs

In addition to finding needlepoint patterns and projects in this book that will fit happily into your home, part of the fun of decorating with needlepoint is making your own custom designs. You may want to duplicate your china pattern on a dining room valance or a section of your living room drapes on a pull-up chair. Perhaps you would like to start your own needlepoint gallery of fine art pictures or posters like the Toulouse Lautrec poster shown here. Line drawings and contemporary art in a geometric or flat decorative style, by such artists as Matisse, Picasso, Frank Stella, and Vasarely translate particularly well into needlepoint.

Use a sheet of clear plastic, called Mylar, which is available from art-supply stores. Lay it over the design you want to copy, and trace the design onto the plastic sheet with a dark marker. Don't try to catch all the details of the original. Include just the main outlines and as much of the detail as can be reproduced on the size canvas you are using (see Figure 9). If you want to extract a detail of a design or one portion of a pattern, trace just that segment on the plastic sheet and ignore the extraneous design. Once you have the design you want, enlarge it and transfer it to the canvas, following the instructions given below (use the same technique to reduce the size of the design).

Figure 9

Enlarging Designs

Regardless of where the design appears—in the pages of this book or another source—you will almost always have to enlarge the design to the size needed for your particular project. The following are three simple methods of enlarging designs without changing their proportions:

Box method. When you want to enlarge the designs in this book, continue drawing the lines that appear on the edges of each color guide until you have divided the entire design into a grid. On a separate large sheet of paper, mark the outline of your finished project and divide the outlined area into the same number of boxes, laid out in the same configuration, that you have drawn over the color guide in the book. You will see that although there are the same number of boxes on each sheet, those on the life-size pattern are much larger. Working box-by-box, transcribe freehand what appears in each design box into the corresponding box of the life-size pattern (see Figure 10). Go over all lines to make them flow smoothly.

For designs from sources other than this book, divide the original design into boxes by drawing a grid over it and follow the procedure explained above.

Photostat. A photocopy store can enlarge (or reduce) a design from this book or most other original sources. Specify the finished size you wish and ask for a positive print—black lines on white paper—rather than the customarily supplied negative print.

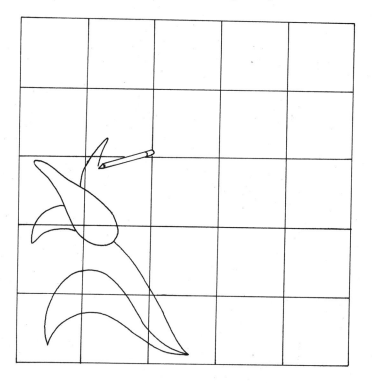

Figure 10

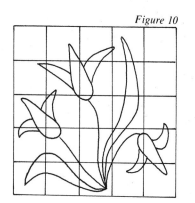

Pantograph. This simple device for reproducing designs is available in art-supply stores. Following manufacturer's directions, set the pantograph to enlarge to required dimensions. While you trace the design with the metal point of the pantograph (it will not make a mark), a pencil, connected by a retractable arm to the point, will duplicate your motions and make an enlargement on a piece of paper.

Extending Designs

Very often, the design you want to stitch will not fit the exact dimensions of your own particular project. In such instances, in addition to enlarging the design, you will also have to extend it. You can do this in one of two ways:

1. Enlarge the design to a size that encompasses your entire project; then trace off that portion of the design that falls within your project boundaries (see Figure 11).

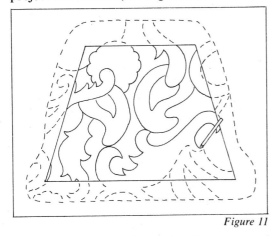

Figure 11

2. Enlarge the design to the size suggested in the book, even though your own project may be larger; then extend the design to fill your project outline by repeating portions of the enlarged design. You can do this either by tracing different sections of the design (see Figure 12) or by "flopping" the outermost parts of the design, thereby extending it without interruption (see Figure 13).

When deciding upon which method to use, remember that method 1 produces a larger-scale design than method 2. Use the one that

Figure 12

Figure 13

seems more appropriate to your design and the scale of your project.

Repeating Designs

Some of the designs in the book, such as those in Section III, are presented in small sections, or "swatches," that are to be repeated rather than enlarged. To do this, first lay a sheet of tracing paper over the book page and trace the design onto it. Then prepare a second piece of tracing paper with the outline of your project. Place the traced design under the larger paper and trace the design onto it. Move the repeat design to an adjacent position and trace the same design again, matching or aligning edges carefully (see Figure 14). Move the design around

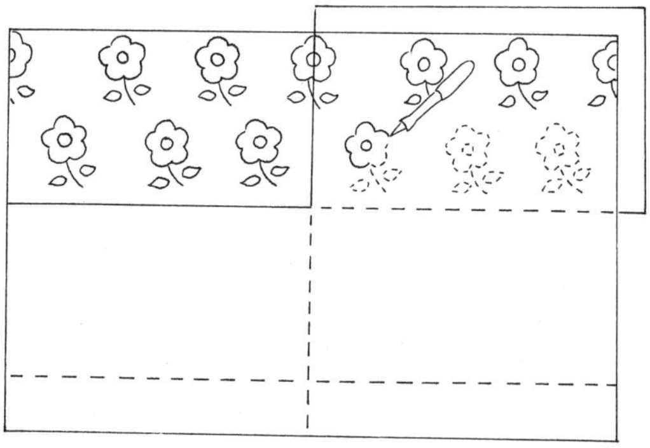

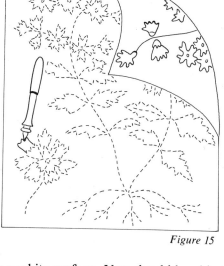

Figure 14

under the larger paper as many times as necessary to fill the outline of your project.

Whatever method you use for enlarging, extending, or repeating designs, go over the finished design with a dark marker so that all lines will be clear enough for transferring them to canvas.

Transferring Designs to Canvas

Once your design is clearly traced on paper in the size you need for your project, it is ready to be transferred to canvas. Center the enlarged design, face up, under the prepared canvas and tape them together. You will be able to see the design clearly enough through the canvas mesh to trace it. If you want to improve the visibility, however, lay the entire piece over a white surface, such as a large piece of white paper, or white sheet. Trace the design onto the canvas with an indelible marker; use a neutral color, never a dark one unless you are working with dark yarns, as dark lines will cast shadows through light-colored stitching. Make absolutely sure that all the markers you use are impervious to both water and dry-cleaning solutions. Remember to check the colorfastness of all markers, even those that claim to be "indelible."

Reverse Designs
You may want to stitch a second project in the mirror image of the first or, perhaps, extract one detail of a design and reverse it. To do this, lay the enlarged design face down

Figure 15

over a white surface. You should be able to see the design clearly enough in order to trace it off on the back of the paper and thereby reverse it (see Figure 15). If you want to improve the visibility, however, tape the enlarged design to a windowpane so that the sun can backlight it.

Graphed Designs
The alphabets, numbers, and a few of the geometric designs in this book are presented on graphs for accuracy. These will not need enlarging, since each intersection of the graph represents an intersection on the canvas. Whenever you are stitching either letters or numbers, be sure to plan that part of your design on graph paper, indicating the spaces to be left between letters and words. Work from your own graph as you stitch (see Figure 16).

Some designs, such as the typewriter cover on page 165, incorporate letters and numbers that will be enlarged when you enlarge the entire design. When you are ready to stitch the letters or numbers, refer to the graphed alphabet in Section III to ensure accuracy.

If you want to center a geometric or bargello pattern, find and mark the center of your canvas by folding the canvas in half

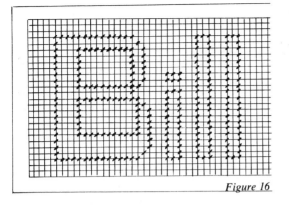

Figure 16

lengthwise and then into quarters. Determine the center of the graphed design and lay out the project accordingly.

Color Guides

Every project in the book is accompanied by a color guide for you to follow. However, you may want to have a more portable color guide to keep in your stitching bag. Here are several possibilities:
● Color code the areas with a paint or crayon or simply pencil in the names of the appropriate colors.
● Tie pieces of your yarn on the canvas to indicate areas of color.
● Paint the entire design on the canvas with acrylic paints. These are available in a wide range of colors, are water-soluble, and won't run or bleed once they have dried. Moreover, a painted canvas won't be obviously visible if any of the stitches fail to cover the mesh completely.

Stitching Designs

The stitches that follow are the ones used in Section II. Most of the projects call for the all-purpose basketweave (or its equivalent—the continental or half cross). The typewriter cover, a sampler of all of the stitches used in this book, shows how much variety is possible within a limited repertoire of stitches and colors. The overcasting stitch is essential for finishing projects on interlocking canvas.

To work the stitches in the following dia-

grams, start with your needle at the back of the canvas; poke it up through the canvas at odd numbers and down through the canvas at even numbers shown on diagram.

Basketweave (Figure 17). This is the all-

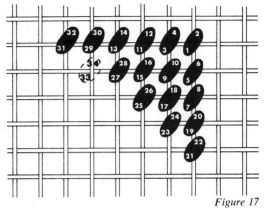

Figure 17

purpose stitch for decorating with needlepoint. It can be worked on mono, penelope, and interlocking canvas. Because of its closely woven crisscross backing, canvas that has been worked in basketweave is supple enough to be upholstered easily and yet has great durability without bulk. Basketweave does not distort the canvas excessively; this makes blocking easier and recommends the stitch for such freestanding projects as wall hangings and rugs that will not be kept in shape by framing or other types of mountings.

Start the stitch in the upper right-hand corner of the design (in the lower left-hand corner if you are left-handed). You will be making your stitches in diagonal rows, rather than along horizontal or vertical threads (see Figure 18); the sequence of stitching follows

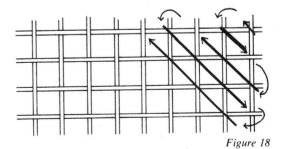

Figure 18

the direction indicated by the arrows. Each individual basketweave stitch is formed in the same way: The thread crosses the intersection of the canvas from the southwest corner to the northeast corner (see Figure

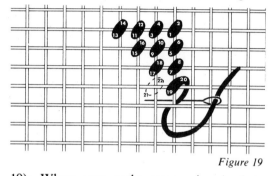

Figure 19

19). When you make successive basketweave stitches in the proper sequence (see Figure 17), the fingering takes on a natural rhythm. Until you have become experienced enough to tell an "up" row from a "down" row by looking at the backing, put needlework aside only when you are in the middle of a row. Insert your needle in the canvas so that it is poised for the next stitch.

Continental (Figure 20). This popular stitch, which looks like basketweave, can be worked on mono, penelope, and interlocking canvas. Continental-stitched canvas is well padded, durable, and facilitates upholstering. However, the stitch distorts the canvas severely, often requiring repeated blockings, and should be avoided for large areas on projects that will not be kept in shape by framing or other mounting. It is most useful for filling in odd-shaped areas of

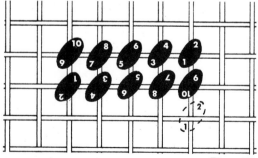

Figure 20

canvas, where the basketweave stitch cannot be easily maintained.

Start at the top of the canvas and work the stitch from right to left across one row; then turn your canvas upside down and stitch the return row in the same manner—that is, from right to left. To reduce canvas tension, which causes distortion, try to keep your stitches slightly slack.

If you are left-handed, start at the bottom of the canvas and work the stitch from left to right; then turn the canvas upside down and work the return row in the same manner—that is, from left to right.

Half Cross (Figure 21). This is another stitch that resembles the basketweave from the front. It is worked on penelope or inter-

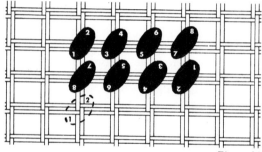

Figure 21

locking canvas but does not hold on mono canvas. Since the half cross is sparsely padded at the back, use it when you don't want bulk and don't anticipate heavy wear. Like the continental, it distorts the canvas badly, often requiring repeated blocking, and should be avoided for large areas. Its principle use is to fill in odd-shaped areas of canvas, where the basketweave stitch cannot easily be maintained.

Start at the top of the canvas and work the half cross from left to right across one row; then turn the canvas upside down and stitch the return row in the same manner—that is, from left to right. Try to keep your stitches slack to reduce the tension on, and therefore, distortion of, the canvas.

If you are left-handed, work the stitch as described above—that is, from left to right across each row—but in this instance start at the bottom of the canvas.

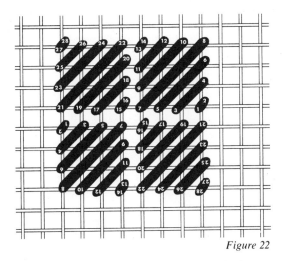

Figure 22

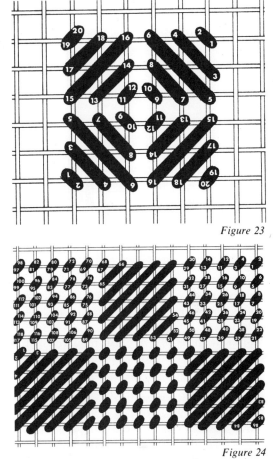

Figure 23

Figure 24

Scotch (Figure 22). The scotch stitch can be worked on mono, penelope, and interlocking canvas. It is more decorative than utilitarian, since its long threads tend to snag. However, it covers the canvas quickly, provides a thick padding on the back, and lends itself to many interesting variations, including a checkerboard design in alternating colors. The scotch stitch pulls the canvas out of shape badly and should be avoided in projects that will not be kept in shape by framing or other mounting. Because the stitch requires that there be a specific number of canvas threads in each direction, you must plan your design ahead.

Start at the top of the canvas and work the stitch from right to left; then turn your canvas upside down and stitch the return row in the same manner—that is, from right to left. Work each stitch sequence over four horizontal and four vertical threads, or over five horizontal and five vertical threads. If you are left-handed, start at the bottom of the canvas and work from left to right; turn the figures upside down for the correct fingering.

You can create a checkerboard effect by stitching contiguous squares in alternating colors, by reversing the slant of contiguous squares (see Figure 23), or by alternating squares of scotch stitch with blocks of basketweave or continental (see Figure 24) in a pattern often called the *checker stitch*.

Gobelin (Figure 25). The gobelin is a simple vertical stitch that can best be worked on mono and interlocking canvas. It covers the canvas quickly without distorting it, making it especially useful for covering large areas. It combines nicely with basketweave, provides sufficient padding to withstand heavy wear, and, when worked over just two canvas threads, is snagproof and supple enough to make upholstering easy.

Start the stitch in the upper right-hand corner of the design. Work one row from right to left and the next row from left to right, always holding the canvas right side up. You can create stripes of varying widths by working the stitch over three, four, or even five horizontal threads and combining

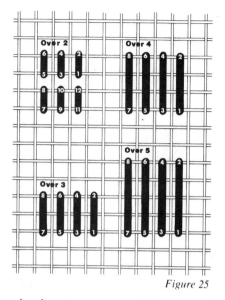

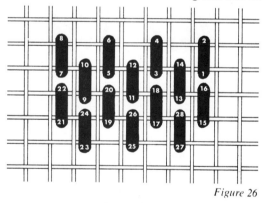

Figure 25

them in the same canvas. If you are left-handed the stitch should be worked in the same way.

Brick (Figure 26). A close relative of the gobelin stitch, the brick stitch can best be worked on mono and interlocking canvas. It

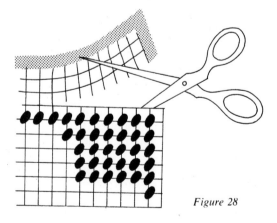

Figure 26

is both decorative and functional: It is closely woven in an attractive bricklike pattern, provides good padding for durability, and covers the canvas quickly without distorting it. It is the most snagproof of the vertical stitches and is excellent for upholstery.

Start the stitch in the upper right-hand corner of the design. Work one row from right to left and the next row from left to right, always holding the canvas right side

up. As you can see, each row of stitches is made in alternate mesh squares and the intervening mesh is filled on the return row, creating a vertical brick pattern. A variation of the stitch can be worked to create a horizontal brick pattern (see Figure 27). The

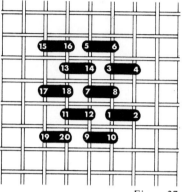

Figure 27

stitches are worked in the same way by left-handers.

Overcasting. The overcasting stitch is used primarily to finish off the cut edges on interlocking canvas. It encroaches into the design area and must be planned for during the work.

After the work has been blocked (see page 28), carefully cut the excess canvas one row outside the existing needlepoint (see Figure 28). Work an overcasting stitch over the cut

Figure 28

edge, including in it both the outer unstitched thread and the last actual stitch (see Figure 29). In order to cover the corners ade-

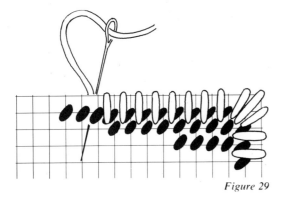

Figure 29

quately, you will have to make at least three overcasting stitches in the corner mesh.

Thread your needle with the same weight yarn used for your design. If you find it doesn't quite cover as you overcast the edge, add another strand to your needle.

When you want the least visible finish to your edges, work the overcasting stitches in the background color. If your background has more than one color, you may want to keep changing yarn color to match. If you want to set off the background or create a border, work the overcasting in a contrasting color.

Tips for Stitching

● An easy way to thread a needle is to double one end of your yarn and loop it over the needle, tucking the needle tightly into the fold. Pinch the fold as you withdraw the needle and thread the doubled yarn through the eye of the needle.

● A good working length of yarn is about 32 inches—just the length you get when you cut a skein of Persian wool twice.

● When starting a new length of yarn, leave an inch or two hanging in the back of the canvas; catch that tail in the back of the next few stitches you make.

● When you have worked down to the last inch or so, tuck the ends of yarn through the backs of neighboring stitches.

● Try to make your stitches fairly loose; work with an even degree of tension to minimize the inevitable distortion.

● As you work, your yarn will tend to become more or sometimes less tightly twisted than it was when you started. To untwist, let the yarn and needle hang loose from the canvas; to retwist, twirl the needle in your fingers. Properly twisted yarn will cover the canvas with plump, durable stitches.

● When making large projects, such as a window valance or shade, roll up those portions of the canvas not presently in work and secure them with large safety pins or extra tapestry needles, taking care not to puncture the canvas threads.

● Stitch central design areas first; you may have to alter the dimensions of the background in order to fit the project.

● Recheck your needlepoint periodically against the project measurements; tight needlework and certain stitches "shrink" the canvas a little. You may have to add some needlepoint around the edges.

● You may find it easier to outline complicated shapes and figures before filling them in. Do this with a series of continental stitches worked in any direction—horizontally, vertically, diagonally—so that in combination they can outline any shape (see

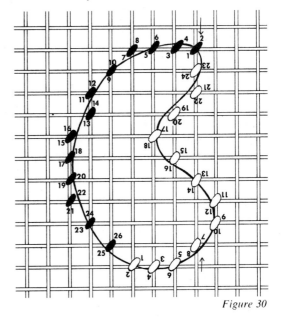

Figure 30

Figure 30). Since the continental and its variations are worked from right to left or from top to bottom, when you want to outline an area that is to the right or above your work area, simply turn the whole canvas upside down; the area you want to outline is now to your left or below your work area (see the white stitches and upside-down numbers in Figure 30).

● When you want to create the appearance of curvilinear lines on the square grid of the canvas, you will have to space, or "step," your stitches so as to create the illusion of a curved line from a distance. In practice, that means that you will make your stitch across the canvas intersection that is closest to the intended curve and that best completes the design. Some stitches may fall inside the design and some outside, but taken in sequence, they will complete the design properly (see Figure 30).

● In counted work, such as bargello and geometrics, always be sure to count rows and stitches rather than to measure with a ruler. Canvas is woven slightly irregularly; 2 inches of No. 10 canvas may have twenty threads along the selvage but twenty-one threads along the horizontal. This discrepancy increases over a large project.

● For continuous change of color without sharp breaks, you can create an ombré look by combining strands of close tones in one thread and gradually replacing them as the overall color changes. For example, to work from dark to light, such as in the rose pillow on page 82, first fill a small area with one 3-strand length of the dark color. Then combine one strand of the lighter shade with two dark strands and stitch another small area. Next, use two light with one dark strand, and, finally, work with three light strands.

● If you run out of yarn before completing one area of color, ease into a new dye lot by combining strands from both old and new dye lots. If you see yourself running short, save a few strands of old yarn for the transition. For example, if you are working with two strands of Persian wool, combine a strand of old with a strand of new yarn until you have used up all the old dye lot.

● When you want to combine large and small stitches on penelope canvas, separate each canvas intersection with your needle into its four smaller components and stitch them with a finer yarn—usually one strand of Persian wool (see Figure 31). When you

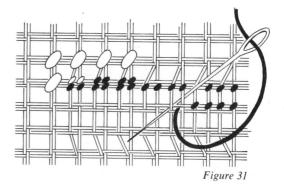

Figure 31

want to resume the large stitch, simply work over the regular penelope intersection without dividing it and switch back to the regular yarn. If there are any areas of background where a full stitch cannot be made, fill in with small stitches in the background color.

● Always tuck a few extra strands of each color yarn into the back of every project to have on hand in case of future repairs. If you clean the needlework, be sure to clean the extra yarn so that it will always match.

● If any canvas shows through your needlepoint, go over the spot with the same stitch and color thread as before; you will probably want to use fewer strands than originally.

● If you want to remove a just-made stitch or two, pull the yarn from the needle, loosen the stitch from the right side of the needlepoint, and pull it out gently. Never poke a threaded needle back through the canvas in the hope of taking out a stitch.

● To reinforce a damaged section of canvas, place a slightly larger piece of identical canvas over it, carefully match both pieces hole-for-hole, baste the intersections together, and then stitch through the two layers of canvas as if they were one (see Figure 32).

● Shield your needlepoint from excessive dirt with a fabric protector, such as Scotchgard. Mist it on lightly a few times, letting it dry thoroughly between applications. Spray the needlepoint after blocking or mounting.

Joining

Many projects require joining, sometimes

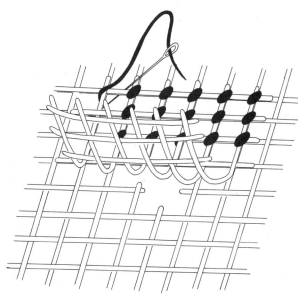

Figure 32

to connect pieces of canvas that are being stitched separately and sometimes to finish cylindrical objects, such as napkin rings and lamp bases.

There are three simple methods of joining canvas, each one of them offering different advantages:

Seam join. A seam join is made on stitched canvas and is sewn in the same manner as any heavy fabric—that is, with right sides together. Use it when you don't need to match a pattern precisely, when you are joining curved sections or canvas of different mesh size, and when you don't know exactly where a seam should fall until after sections have been stitched, blocked, and fitted. Although it creates a little extra bulk and is the most visible join, it is the easiest to make and offers the most flexibility.

A seam join is made inside a seam allowance of at least two rows of needlepoint. The seam allowance can be deeper than two rows but should not be less.

Block needlepoint sections to be joined (see page 28); then protect all edges to be seamed with a row of machine stitching.

Place the two sections of needlepoint with right sides together; baste along the seam line, carefully matching the rows (see Figure 33); then sew by machine. Cut away the excess canvas and masking tape, leaving about 1 inch of unworked canvas (see Figure 34). Turn the seam open and tack the excess canvas to the back of the needlepoint (see Figure 35).

Overlap join. An overlap join is made by stitching through two layers of unstitched canvas. Use it when you want an almost invisible join and when you want to continue a design without interruption. It must be used with canvas of the same size mesh and should be planned for from the start.

On each edge to be joined, work your design to within 2 or 3 inches of the design outline. On the right or top section, carefully cut the canvas just outside the design outline (see Figure 36). Glue the cut edge with all-

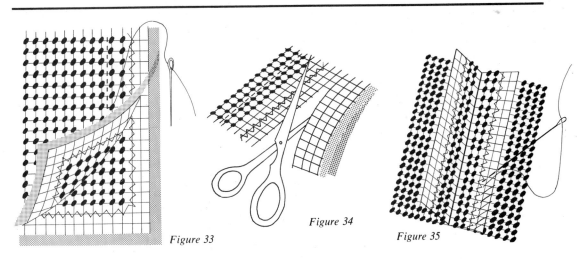

Figure 33

Figure 34

Figure 35

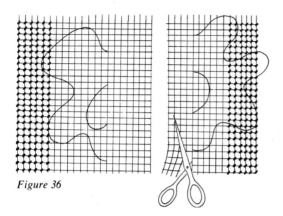

Figure 36

purpose white glue and let dry.

On the left or bottom section, count five mesh outside the design outline; carefully cut the canvas between the fifth and sixth threads (see Figure 37). Apply glue to this cut edge and let dry.

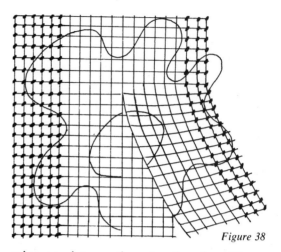

Figure 38

ering one intersection at a time (see Figure 39). Continue to stitch your needlepoint

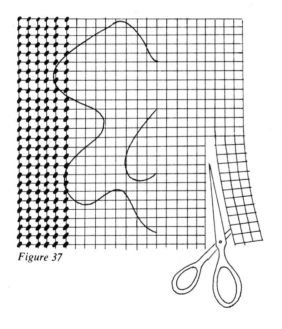

Figure 37

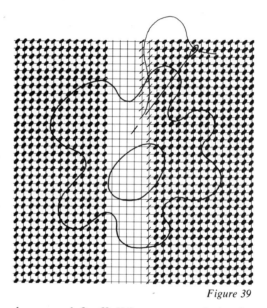

Figure 39

Place the unstitched threads of the right or top section over those of the left or bottom section so that the outlines of the design meet, continuing the pattern without a break (see Figure 38). Match the canvas mesh and baste them together with carpet thread, cov-

where you left off. When you reach the doubled canvas, stitch through it as if it were a single layer (see Figure 40), continuing the same stitch you have been using. When working on the double canvas, you will probably find it easier to make your stitches with two separate motions—down and then up—instead of one continuous movement. Continue stitching until the design is joined.

When using the basketweave or conti-

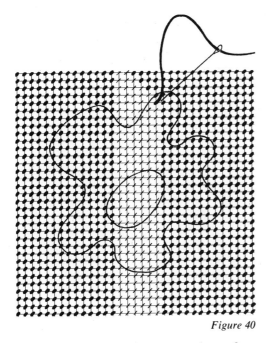

Figure 40

nental stitch, take the precaution of anchoring the cut edge of the upper canvas with a cross-stitch to cover the raw end that may pop out (see Figure 41). Stitch the overlying stroke of the cross in the same direction as the other stitches.

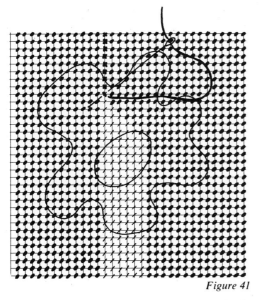

Figure 41

Butt join. A butt join is made by whipping the outermost thread of each side together in a single row. Although not as strong as the other two joins, it is fairly invisible. Its best

use is for completing cylindrical objects that won't get much wear.

First, block the needlepoint piece to be finished (see page 28) and protect the edges to be joined with a row of machine stitching. Cut away the excess canvas and masking tape along the edges to be joined, leaving about 1 inch of unstitched canvas (see Figure 42).

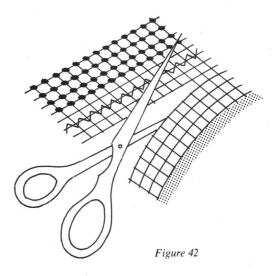

Figure 42

On each side, turn the excess canvas to the back, leaving just one row of canvas thread showing (see Figure 43). Butt the two

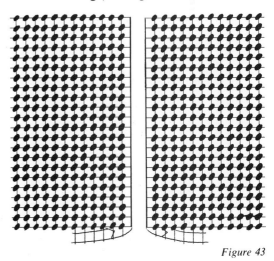

Figure 43

sides: With carpet thread, baste the two outer rows together, matching rows and stitching so that the two sides are secure and don't move back and forth (see Figure 44).

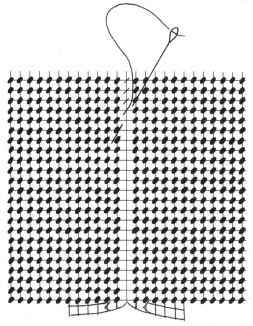

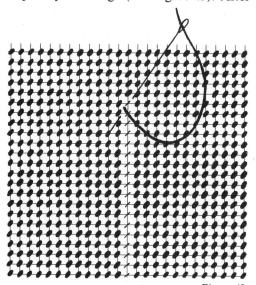

Figure 44

Using appropriate color yarn, work over the basted row in a vertical outline stitch to complete your design (see Figure 45). After

Figure 45

joining, hem the excess canvas to the back of the needlepoint (see Figure 46).

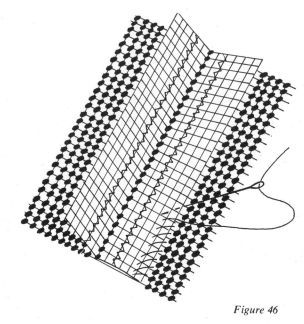

Figure 46

Blocking

Virtually every piece of needlepoint will have to be blocked when completed; the tug of the diagonal stitches on the canvas threads pulls the piece out of shape. The only exception may be bargello work, where the vertical stitches don't exert a distorting pull on the canvas.

Blocking boards should be strong enough to provide proper tension for blocking, yet soft enough for tacks to penetrate easily. Of course, they should also be large enough to hold your project. Wallboard and various other dense composition boards, as well as softwood boards, such as pine, are available from lumberyards and are excellent.

Tack your brown paper guide with its canvas outline (see page 14) right onto the blocking board. If you want an allover ruled guide, first cover the blocking board with a geometric cotton print, such as a plaid. Lay the fabric out evenly and pull it taut over all four sides of the board; then staple it to the underside.

To restore the canvas to its original shape, both canvas and stitching must be damp; a badly distorted canvas needs more soaking than one that is slightly askew. For severe distortion, roll the needlepoint in a damp towel and let the water penetrate before tacking to the blocking board. Fairly straight work can be put on the blocking board while it is still dry and then sprayed with tepid water or a steam iron.

Whether the needlepoint is damp or dry, lay it face down on the brown paper. Match the register marks at the two corners and the center of the top edge with the corresponding register marks on the brown paper; anchor the two corners of the canvas with stainless steel T-pins or any other rustproof tacks, pinning through the taped edge of the canvas (see Figure 47). Avoid tacking through

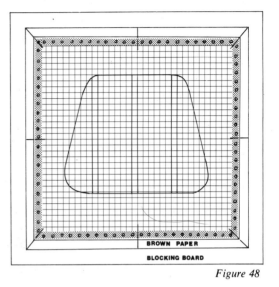

Figure 48

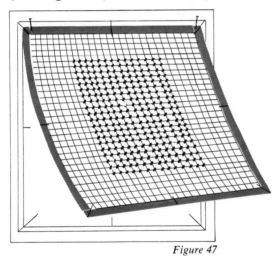

Figure 47

stitches if taped or unworked canvas is available.

If you have not yet moistened the needlepoint, do so at this time. Once the needlepoint is damp and pliable, you will be able to pull the third and fourth corners into shape to conform to the outline on the brown paper. When the register marks on the paper and the canvas match, tack the needlepoint every inch or so along the sides and at the corners (see Figure 48). With a severely distorted canvas, you may have to coax a stubborn side into shape gradually, tacking and re-

tacking several times and spraying the needlepoint repeatedly to make it more pliant. When the piece has been tacked all around, let it dry horizontally for several days.

Tips for Blocking
• Keep your needlepoint on the blocking board until you are ready to mount it so that the canvas can't creep back out of shape. Tacks at the four corners are sufficient.

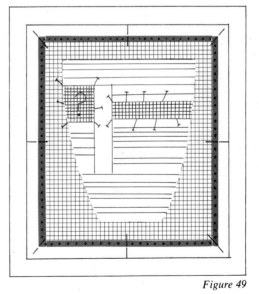

Figure 49

● Samplers incorporate various stitches that may pull in different directions; these internal areas of distortion have to be blocked separately. Insert stainless steel T-pins into the canvas mesh around each area of distortion, taking care not to split the yarn or canvas threads (see Figure 49).

● Severely distorted work may have to be blocked repeatedly. When finishing such projects, try to mount them on a rigid surface or back them with tightly woven fabrics.

Protecting Edges

Whenever you finish or mount a piece of needlepoint, you will have to cut away the masking tape that binds the edges, as well as any excess canvas that may make the finished project bulky. But cut canvas tends to ravel, eventually endangering your needlepoint stitches. You can protect them in one or both of the following ways:

Machine stitching. Sew a row of machine stitching just outside the edge of the needlepoint (see Figure 50). If your machine doesn't zigzag, make two parallel rows of stitching.

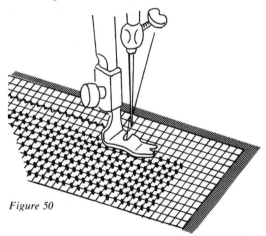

Figure 50

Gluing. Apply a thin line of all-purpose white glue at the edge of the cut canvas or about ½ inch out from the edge of the needlepoint (see Figure 51). The exact location will depend on the needs of your particular project. The white glue dries colorless and

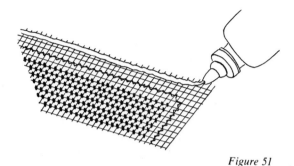

Figure 51

will not harm the needlepoint.

Squeeze the glue from the special applicator head to form a thin line. If you find that the glue beads up, spread it with a toothpick, keeping the film as thin as possible. Let the glue dry thoroughly before resuming work. Clear any mesh that might become clogged with glue by piercing it with the point of your needle.

Mitering Corners

A great variety of projects rely on mitered corners for a trim, neat look. Sometimes the miter is made over a stiff backing board, as with framed needlepoint, mirror or picture frames, bulletin boards, and tabletops. In other projects, such as wall hangings and rugs, the miter is made right over the back of the needlepoint. In either case, the mitering technique is the same. Note, however, that when the miter is made over a backing board, you must provide two to four rows of extra stitching around the sides (the exact number of rows will depend on the thickness of the board), while one row of extra stitching is sufficient when no backing board is used.

Before mitering, block the needlepoint (see page 28). Sew a row of machine stitching on the excess canvas about ¼ inch outside the needlepoint. This will protect the soon-to-be-cut canvas edges from raveling. Cut the excess canvas away on all four sides to within 1½ inches of the needlepoint; cut the corners diagonally to within ½ inch of the corner point (see Figure 52). On small or narrow projects, such as the luggage-rack straps on page 137, you may want to reduce

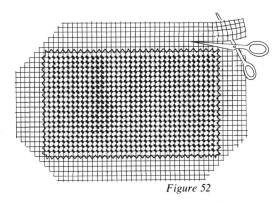

Figure 52

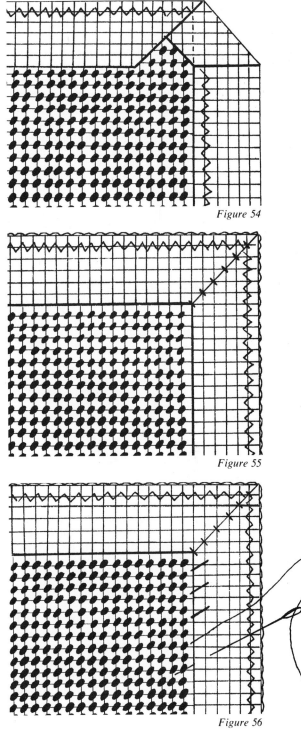

Figure 54

Figure 55

the width of this excess canvas "hem." If, however, you cut to within four canvas threads of the finished needlepoint, be sure to apply a thin line of glue just inside the cut edges as a second line of defense against potential raveling.

To do the actual mitering of the corners, lay the needlepoint face down on a table. At one corner, turn the diagonal edge back until it just meets the corner stitching (see Figure 53). Then turn each adjoining side over the

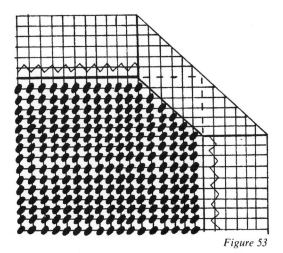

Figure 53

back of the needlepoint (see Figure 54). Whip the mitered corner together neatly (see Figure 55). Repeat for the other corners. Tack the turned-back canvas to the back of the stitched needlepoint with carpet thread, making sure that the rows of stitching are straight and that no excess canvas shows along the edges (see Figure 56).

Figure 56

To miter corners over a rigid backing, lay the blocked needlepoint—after the excess canvas has been cut away—face down on a table; center the rigid board over it. Temporarily anchor the needlepoint to the edge of the board with T-pins or tacks, making sure that the rows of stitching are straight. On fairly thick plywood, you can tack the needlepoint to the edge of the board (see Figure 57a); on cardboard, anchor the needlepoint

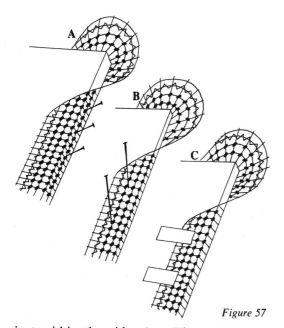

Figure 57

just within the sides (see Figure 57b); on Masonite, hold the needlepoint in place temporarily with masking tape (see Figure 57c). Miter the corners as described above; then secure the sides according to the instructions in each project.

Lacing

Lacing is a useful way to hold needlepoint taut against rigid surfaces that cannot easily be glued—plywood, Masonite, and metal. While most often used in conjunction with mitered corners, it is useful in other circumstances as well, such as tightening needlepoint across the bottom of upholstered chairs and tables.

Before lacing, block the needlepoint (see page 28) and protect its edges (see page 30) by both machine stitching and gluing (see Figure 58). Lay the prepared needlepoint

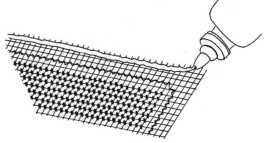

Figure 58

face down and position the rigid backing over it, making sure that the rows of needlepoint are straight. Using heavy carpet thread and a curved upholsterer's needle if possible, lace opposite edges of the canvas together, working from the center toward the corners. Insert the needle from the top and bring it through between the last two rows of stitching (see Figure 59). Do not lace into the

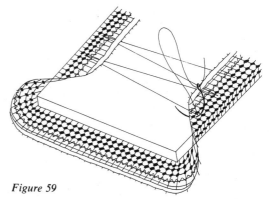

Figure 59

raw canvas threads. If it is not feasible to lace into finished needlepoint, insert the lacing thread into canvas mesh within the area that has been protected by the machine stitching and glue. Never lace into unprotected canvas; the tension of the lacing thread may ravel the weave of the mesh.

Work to within 2 or 3 inches of each corner; then secure the carpet thread and lace the other pair of edges together in the same manner (see Figure 60). Finish the cor-

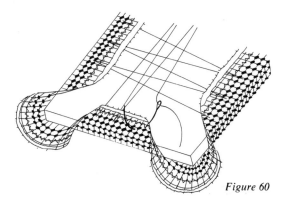

Figure 60

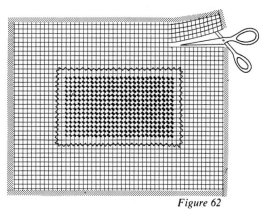

Figure 62

ners according to the instructions given with the project; complete lacing opposite sides together.

If you want a finished underside, blind-stitch a lining or glue felt or heavy paper over the lacing (see Figure 61).

With the needlepoint face down, turn the cut canvas edges over the finished stitches, pulling tightly so that no raw canvas shows from the side (see Figure 63). Tack the edges

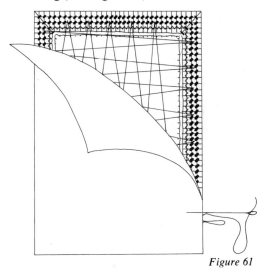

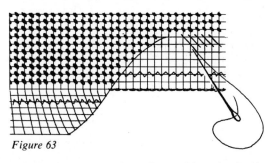

Figure 63

down with carpet thread, catching the back of the needlepoint stitches.

You can give your needlepoint added body by interlining it with buckram. Cut the buckram to the precise size of the finished project; baste it to the back of the blocked needlepoint, securing it through the back of the needlepoint stitches (see Figure 64). If it

Figure 61

Hemming

Many needlepoint projects have to be hemmed during the course of finishing. Sew a row of machine stitching along the sides to be hemmed, about ¼ inch outside the nee-dlepoint. Then cut away the excess canvas and the masking tape to within 1½ inches of the needlepoint (see Figure 62). On small or narrow projects, you may want to reduce the width of this canvas hem.

Figure 64

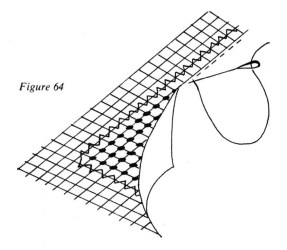

is a large piece, tack it in several places. Hem the canvas as described above, being sure to catch the back of the needlepoint stitches as well as the interlining.

If you are hemming a piece of needlepoint with inside or outside curves, notch the raw canvas. Always leave at least one canvas thread to protect the needlepoint and safeguard it further with a row of machine stitching (see Figure 65).

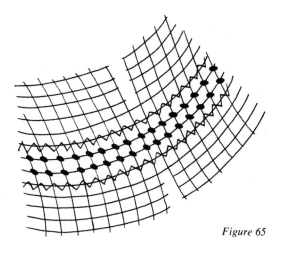

Figure 65

Lining

Lining is usually the last of the finishing operations, done after the needlepoint has been blocked, hemmed, or otherwise finished. It lends a trim and tidy look to the back and masks any unsightly ends or raw canvas.

Linings should be made of tightly woven material. The easiest materials to work with are those that need no further hemming—ribbons of all kinds and felt, which is particularly useful for irregular shapes. Cut felt about ¼ inch smaller than the finished article and blindstitch in place (see Figure 66). Choose grosgrain or other ribbon of appropriate width for narrow projects, such as the tray hanger on page 152, and blindstitch in place. (*Note:* Try to have the lining ribbon on hand before starting the project so that you will be able to adjust the width of the project to the ribbon, if necessary.)

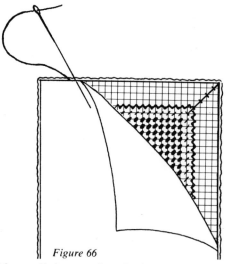

Figure 66

If your lining needs to be hemmed, cut it ½ inch larger all around than the finished needlepoint. Lay the needlepoint face down on a flat surface with the lining material over it, face up. Tack or pin the lining to the needlepoint in a few places to anchor it temporarily. Starting at the top, turn the ½-inch hem under so that the lining will come just to the edge of the needlepoint; miter each top corner of the lining and blindstitch it in place (see Figure 67). Work around the two sides

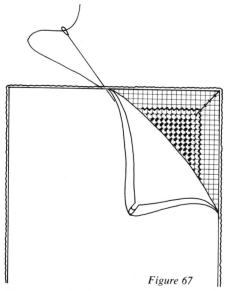

Figure 67

and bottom, mitering the corners of the lining as you come to them. Remove the pins or tacking.

Edgings

Edgings of various kinds—welting, cording, ruffles, tassels—give most projects a professional finish. Commercial edgings of all kinds are available, and the fabric cording that can't be made by hand is especially welcome. But the most elegant edgings are those that use the yarns of the needlepoint and the fabrics of the backing or boxing strip.

Welting. Welting is made from 1½-inch strips of fabric. You will have to piece a long strip from shorter strips; 1 square yard of fabric will yield about 24 yards of strips that have been cut on the bias. Make the strip as follows: Lay the fabric on the table and place the crosswise threads evenly along the lengthwise threads (see Figure 68). The re-

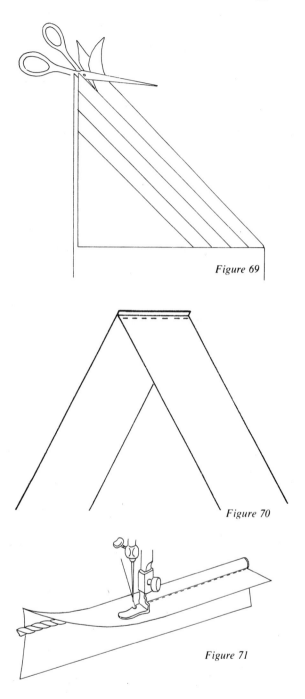

Figure 69

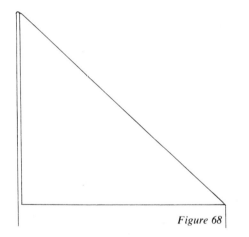

Figure 68

Figure 70

sulting diagonal fold will run along the true bias. Cut along this fold; then cut 1½-inch-wide strips parallel to the fold cut (see Figure 69). Join the strips by seaming across the short end (lengthwise grain) with right sides together (see Figure 70). Continue joining the strips into one length until the required length is reached.

To turn the long strip into welting, place the strip right side down and lay cotton cording (available at notions or sewing centers) along the center. Bring the two sides of the strip together and, with the zipper foot of your sewing machine, seam as close to the cording as possible (see Figure 71).

Figure 71

The general procedure for attaching welting to needlepoint is as follows: Along all edges to be welted, machine-stitch a row just outside the needlepoint. To minimize the eventual welting join, start the welting in an inconspicuous place—the middle of the back or bottom edge, for instance. Lay the blocked canvas face up; place the welting over it, with the unfinished edge of the bias strip pointed toward the masking tape and the corded side over the finished needlepoint. The seam of the welting should be directly over the desired join. This will usually be just inside the two extra rows of needlepoint, which will be referred to as the seam allowance (see Figure 72). Baste and then,

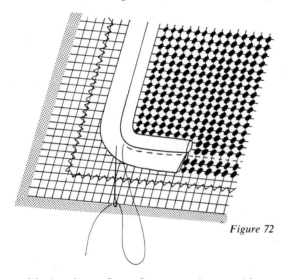

Figure 72

with the zipper foot of your sewing machine, sew along the seam of the welting. As you come to curves or corners, notch the bias strip (see Figure 73).

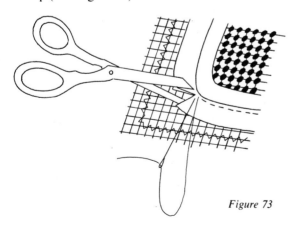

Figure 73

When you want to attach welting all around a project, join the ends of the welting as follows: Stop seaming the welting to the needlepoint a few inches short of the desired join. Cut the right end of the welting so that it will overlap the join by 1 inch (see Figure 74). On that end, open up the last inch of the

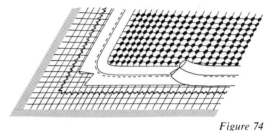

Figure 74

seam and cut off 1 inch of the cording so that it will abut the cording in the left end when joined (see Figure 75). Turn under ¼ inch at the end of the now-unseamed bias strip, and

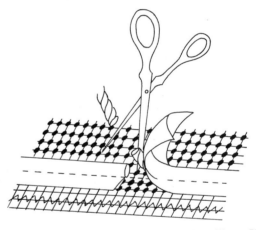

Figure 75

tuck it around the welting on the left end (see Figure 76). Continue to seam the welting on the right to the needlepoint, stitching over the doubled strip where the cording abuts at the join.

Either a backing fabric or a boxing strip (see page 40) will be sewn to the welted needlepoint. Place right sides together and sew on top of the welting seam line (see Figure 77 and 90).

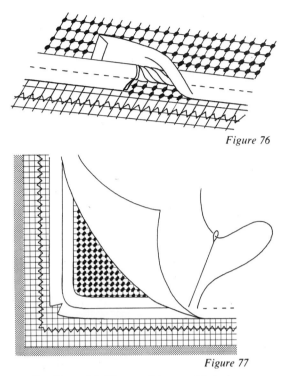

Figure 76

Figure 77

yarn pulled taut, twist the pencil in the same direction that the yarn is already twisted (see Figure 79). As you turn to form a tighter

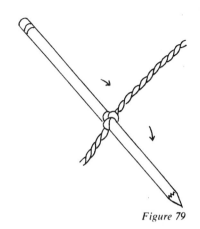

Figure 79

twist, keep the yarn taut to avoid kinking. Once the yarn has been tightly twisted, grab the center knot in one hand while still holding the pencil in the other. Keeping the yarn extended and held taut, slip the knot on the pencil off and onto the hook or nail (see Figure 80). Gradually relax the yarn at the

Cording. Unlike welting, which is sewn right into the seam, cording is applied over a finished seam as a decorative trim. You can buy fabric cording, or you can make your own cording from yarn in the following way: Cut a piece of yarn that is three times the length of the required cording. Make a knot in the center; tie one end of the yarn to a nail or hook on the wall and the other to a pencil (see Figure 78). Hold the pencil and, with the

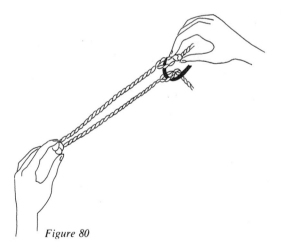

Figure 80

center knot; it will form tightly twisted cording about twice the thickness of the original yarn. Tie the two end knots together (see Figure 81).

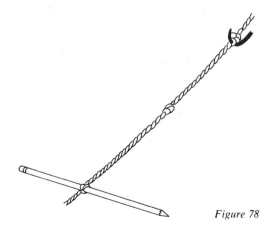

Figure 78

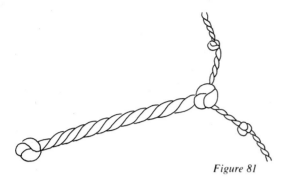

Figure 81

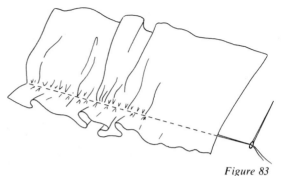

Figure 83

Sew the cording over a finished seam with blindstitches (see Figure 82). On upholstered

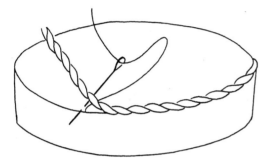

Figure 82

pieces, such as a headboard or chair, you can attach the cording with any all-purpose white glue if it is too difficult a task to blindstitch it.

Ruffles. A ruffled edge makes a charming finish for pillows or cushions of any shape and is particularly appropriate for informal settings or dainty designs. The edging is sewn between the needlepoint and the backing fabric in exactly the same manner and position as the welting.

The easiest materials to ruffle are ribbons because they already have two selvaged edges, but any strip of material can be gathered. Choose a strip of fabric, 2 to 3 or more inches wide (depending on the size and scale of your project) and 2 to 2½ times as long as the perimeter, circumference, or side to be ruffled. Sew a basting stitch about ¼ inch in from one long edge; then pull your thread to create the ruffle (see Figure 83). Gather the strip to the length you need and distribute the gathers evenly.

To attach the ruffle, lay the blocked needlepoint face up; place the gathered strip over it, ruffles pointing in and gathered seam directly over the needlepoint seam allowance. Baste and then sew the ruffle to the needlepoint on top of the gathered seam (see Figure 84). When the ruffle is attached all around, join its ends together.

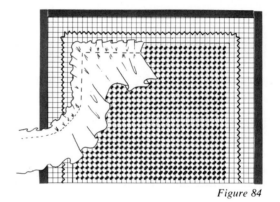

Figure 84

Place the ruffled needlepoint and the backing fabric right sides together. Baste and then sew over the seam, leaving an 8-inch opening for inserting an inner pillow, if desired, and for turning right side out.

Tassels. Tassels are a nice way to finish off the corners of rectangular pillows and some wall hangings. They can be used alone or with welted or corded seams. They are usually most elegant when they are made from the same yarns that were used in the projects, although not necessarily with all the same colors.

Cut two 9-inch pieces of yarn and put them aside. Wind the body of the tassel around a piece of cardboard, 4 to 5 inches long (see

Figure 85); if you want a longer tassel, use larger cardboard. Wrap the yarn around the

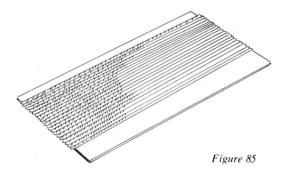

Figure 85

board about twenty times for a fairly thin tassel and about forty times for a more luxuriant tassel.

Tie one of the 9-inch lengths of yarn around the wound yarn at the center (see Figure 86); remove the cardboard. Knot the

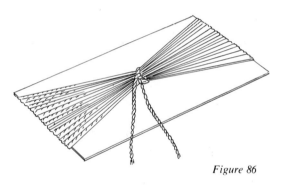

Figure 86

second 9-inch length of yarn around the body of the tassel, 1 to 1½ inches below the other knot, to make a head. Let the yarn ends fall in with the body of the tassel. Cut the yarn at the bottom and even off the strands if necessary (see Figure 87).

You can mount the finished tassel close to the corners of the project by inserting the top tie into the corner seam as you sew it (see Figure 88). Or, you can incorporate the top tie into a braid or cording so that the tassel will hang some distance from the project (see Figure 89). Two tassels finished with a long braid can be used to tie a cushion on a chair, as shown in the child's-chair on page 57.

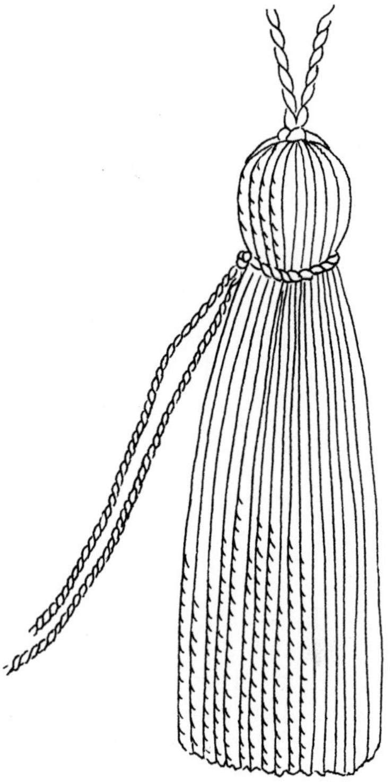

Figure 87

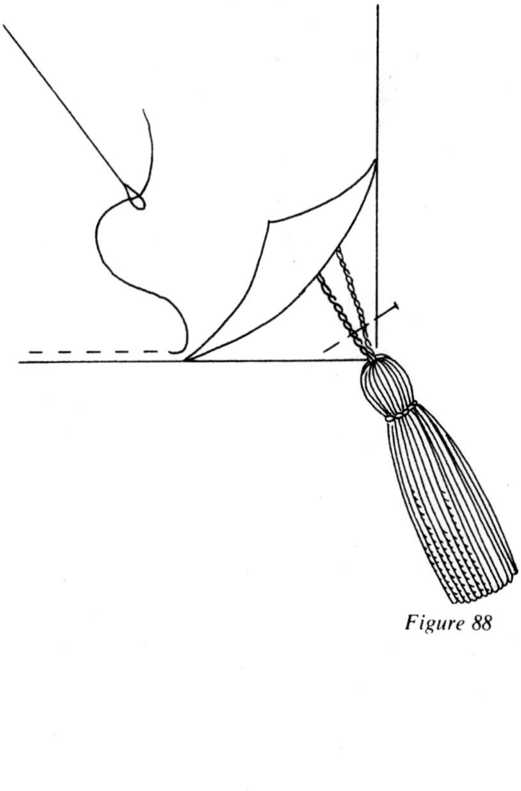

Figure 88

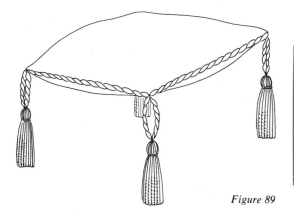

Figure 89

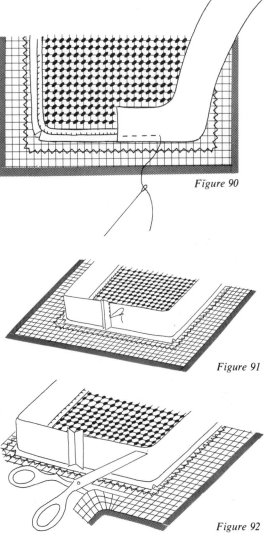

Figure 90

Figure 91

Figure 92

Boxing Strips

A boxed pillow or cushion gives a trim, tailored look to finished needlepoint. The strip is usually made in the same fabric as the backing, although it may be in a coordinate fabric or even in needlepoint; it is also usually used with welting. Its length is the perimeter or circumference of the pillow or cushion plus a ½-inch seam allowance at each end. Its width is optional and can range from 1 inch for a thin chair pad to 8 or more inches (plus ½-inch seam allowances on either side) for a floor pillow. A needlepoint boxing strip requires two extra rows of stitching on all four edges in place of the seam allowance.

If both the needlepoint and backing are to be welted (see page 35), complete these procedures before attaching the boxing strip.

Lay the welted needlepoint face up on a table. Starting in the middle of the back or bottom of the project, place the right side of the boxing strip over it, face down, so that the seam allowance of the boxing strip lies directly over the seam of the welting (see Figure 90). Baste and then sew the strip to the welted needlepoint around the sides, notching the corners. When you reach your starting point, join the two ends of the boxing strip (see Figure 91).

With the project still inside out, trim the excess canvas to within ½ inch of the needlepoint and cut the corners diagonally (see Figure 92).

Lay the welted fabric backing face up and, with the project still inside out, place the seam allowance of the boxing strip directly over the seam allowance of the welted backing. Baste the pieces together; then sew over the welting seam, starting at one end of the back edge. Sew around all four corners, notching the boxing strip at each corner. Stop sewing just after you turn the last corner, leaving most or enough of the back seam open to enable you to stuff easily (see Figure 93); turn right side out.

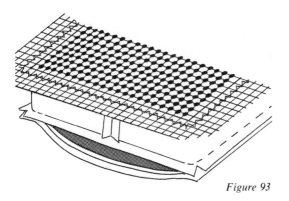

Figure 93

Stuff with an inner box pillow or slab of foam rubber. Blindstitch the back opening (see Figure 94).

Inner Pillows

For a trim and tailored look, fill your pillow with a flat slab of foam rubber. A 1-inch thickness is appropriate for a thin chair pad, 8 or more inches for a hassock-type floor pillow. Have the foam cut to the full dimensions of your project.

For a plump or informal look, make an inner pillow out of muslin to the same size and shape as your needlepoint pillow. Leave an opening in one of the seams and stuff well with down, shredded foam rubber, polyester fiberfill, or Dacron. When the pillow is nicely plump, the filling evenly distributed, and the corners well padded, blindstitch the open seam (see Figure 95).

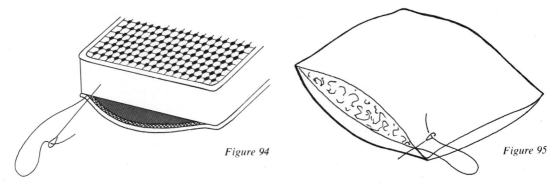

Figure 94

Figure 95

Needlepoint for the Home

A galaxy of furnishings—chairs, benches, tables, decorative accessories of all kinds—await you in this section. Each project has been designed to light up even the most unlikely corners of your home. The projects are presented in a uniform format that specifies the stitch, the canvas, and the amount of yarn to be used, plus any additional materials that may be required. Instructions for enlarging and tracing designs, special tips for working each article, and detailed finishing and assembling directions follow.

Also, you will see how to adapt designs to your own chair, table, or accessory, if it has different dimensions. Finally, the added fillip of the "Decorating Bonus" helps you get the most enjoyment out of decorating with needlepoint.

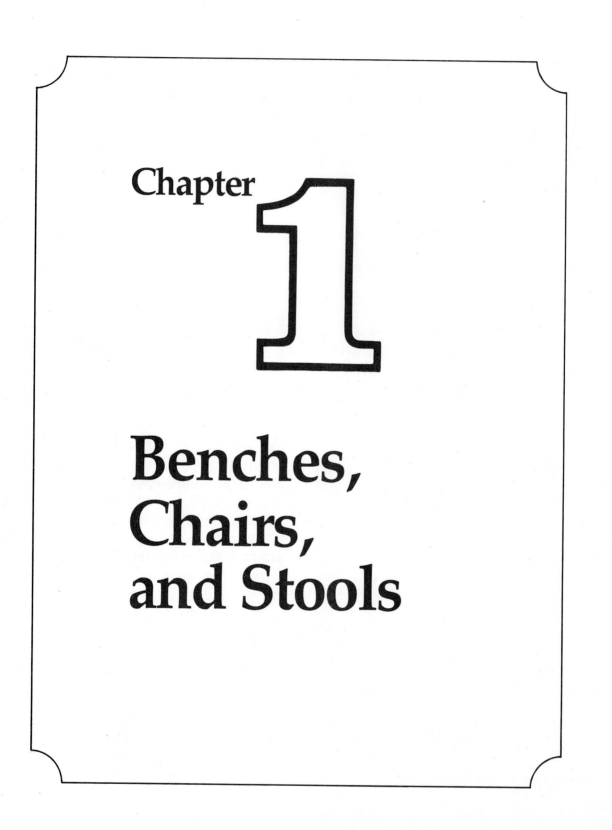

Chapter **1**

Benches, Chairs, and Stools

French Provincial Chair Pad

A charming French provincial fabric was the inspiration for this side chair cushion. This particular chair pad is 17 inches deep, 20 inches wide across the front, and 15½ inches wide across the back. The design, however, can easily be adapted to any chair measurements. The pad is finished in the same way as a box cushion and is tied to the chair with fabric strips.

To make this French provincial chair pad, you will be using the following basic procedures, which have been described in detail in Section I:

- Preparing canvas
- Enlarging designs
- Transferring designs to canvas
- Stitching designs
- Blocking
- Protecting edges
- Welting
- Making boxing strips
- Making inner pillows

Stitch

Basketweave

Canvas

No. 12 mono
Cut one piece 20 by 24 inches, and bind the edges with masking tape.

Yarn

You will need about 8 ounces of Persian wool; about 5 ounces of it will be used for the background.

Additional Materials

fabric backing, ½ inch larger all around than the finished needlepoint
boxing strip, 2½ inches wide and 1 inch longer than the perimeter of the needlepoint (about 64 inches)

Design derived from the pattern "Villandry"© Comptoir de l'Industrie Textile de France, available through Boussac of France, New York.

2 strips of welting, each the length of the boxing strip
2 fabric strips for ties, each to measure 24 inches long and about ¾ inch wide when finished
inner box pillow to fit

Enlarging and Transferring

Enlarge the design so that the depth at the center measures 17 inches; the width at the widest part will be about 20 inches. Center the enlarged design face up under the canvas and, using an indelible marker, trace it onto the canvas.

Special Tips for Work

Around all four edges, extend the design two additional rows to provide for a seam allowance.

Finishing and Assembling

Block the needlepoint.

Sew a row of machine stitching on the excess canvas just outside the needlepoint.

Lay the needlepoint face up. Starting at the middle of the back edge, place the welting over the needlepoint so that its unfinished edge is pointed out toward the taped canvas edge and the seam of the welting is directly over the needlepoint seam allowance. Baste and then sew them together on top of the welting seam, notching the welting strip as you turn the corners (see Figure 73). When the welting is attached all around, join the ends and seam it to the needlepoint (see Figure 76).

Place the fabric backing face up. Fold the fabric ties in half; pin them over the two rear corners of the backing, with loose ends facing in and loop extending out about 1 inch. Sew the second strip of welting to the face of the backing, leaving a ½-inch seam allowance (just as you welted the needlepoint). When you come to each rear corner, simply sew the welting over the fabric ties (see Figure 1).

Lay the needlepoint face up; starting at the middle of the back edge, place the boxing strip face down so that its seam allowance lies directly over the seam of the welting. Baste and then sew the boxing strip to the welted needlepoint around the four sides, notching the corners when you come to them (see Figure 2). When you reach your starting point, join the two ends of the boxing strip. Trim the unstitched canvas to within ½ inch of the needlepoint and cut the corners diagonally (see Figure 3).

Lay the welted fabric backing face up.

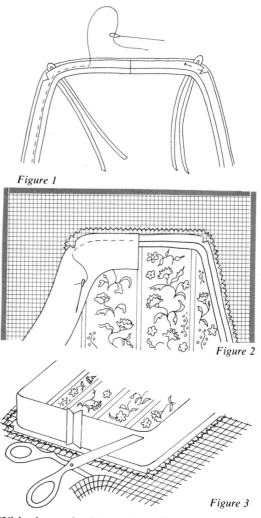

Figure 1

Figure 2

Figure 3

With the welted boxed needlepoint still inside out, place the seam allowance of the boxing strip directly over the seam allowance of the welted backing. Baste and then sew the boxing strip to the welted backing; start at one rear corner and stop just after you have turned the last corner, leaving most or enough of the back seam open for stuffing (see Figure 4).

Turn right side out, stuff with inner box pillow, and blindstitch the back opening (see Figure 5).

Adjusting the Design Area

If the cushion does not fit your particular chair, outline your chair seat on a piece of canvas. Enlarge the design to accommodate

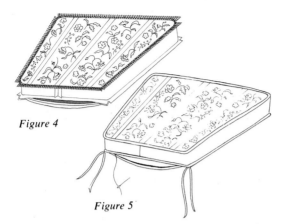

Figure 4

Figure 5

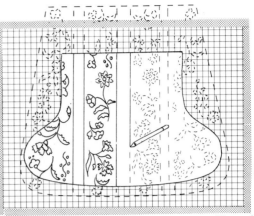

Figure 6

the largest dimension of your seat. Center the enlarged design face up under the canvas and trace onto the canvas that portion of the design that falls within the chair seat outline (see Figure 6).

Decorating Bonus

For the backing fabric and boxing strip, choose a coordinating fabric already used in the room.

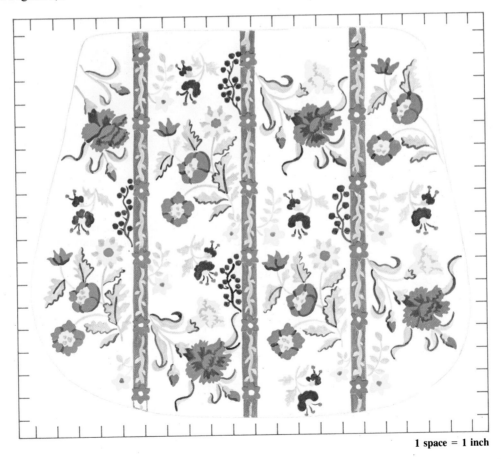

1 space = 1 inch

Geometric-Repeat Chair Seat

The contemporary geometric pattern on this slip seat contrasts nicely with the Chippendale armchair it covers. A slip-seated chair is easy to refurbish. Usually, you can simply unscrew the seat panel and remove the existing upholstery, which will then become the custom pattern for your needlepoint. When you have finished, the slip seat-cover can be tacked in the same way as the original. In some instances, you may have to replace worn-out padding.

To make the geometric-design slip seat, you will be using the following basic procedures, which have been described in detail in Section I:

- Preparing canvas
- Making custom patterns
- Transferring designs to canvas
- Stitching designs
- Blocking
- Protecting edges

Stitch

Basketweave

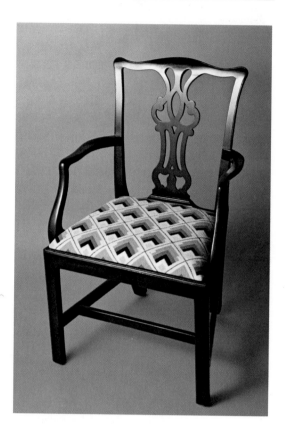

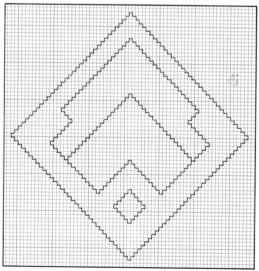

Figure 1

Canvas

No. 12 or No. 13 mono

Cut one piece of canvas so that it is 2 inches larger all around than the dimensions of your chair seat, and bind the edges with masking tape.

Yarn

You will need almost 1 ounce of Persian wool for each diamond repeat shown in Figure 1.

Additional Materials

cambric for lining, ½ inch larger all around than the bottom of the seat

Enlarging and Transferring

Make a custom pattern for your own seat, and trace its outline onto canvas with an indelible marker. Center the pattern on the canvas and fill the area within the outline with repeat design (see Figure 2).

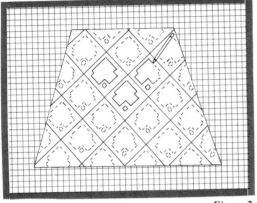

Figure 2

Special Tips for Work

On all four sides, extend the design 1½ inches beyond the seat area to accommodate the padding and turn-under.

Finishing and Assembling

Block the needlepoint.

Sew a row of machine stitching on the excess canvas just outside the needlepoint.

Cut the excess canvas away on all sides to within 1½ inches of the stitching, and cut the corners diagonally to within 1 inch of the stitching.

Remove the existing cambric and upholstery from the seat panel; replace padding if needed.

Lay the needlepoint face down on your work surface. Over it, center the seat panel so that its padded side faces the needlepoint. Temporarily anchor the needlepoint at the center of each side by tacking it to the seat panel (see Figure 3).

Permanently secure the right and left sides by nailing short upholstery tacks through the

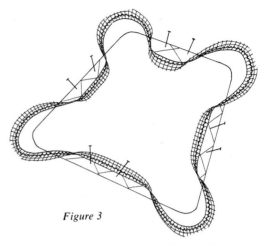

Figure 3

edge of the needlepoint. Work from the center out toward the corners, tacking every inch or so and pulling the needlepoint taut as you work.

Tack the front edge to the panel in the same manner, working from the center out toward the sides. At each corner, ease the needlepoint into neat folds (see Figure 4).

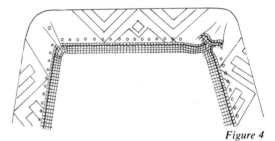

Figure 4

Tack the back edge of the seat in the same manner as the sides and front. If your corners are more rounded than angular, you will have to take up the fullness with a number of narrow pleats; secure them with closely spaced tacks (see Figure 5). Cut away any

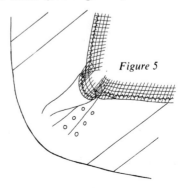

Figure 5

excess canvas to reduce bulk, gluing the cut edges if necessary.

Lay the cambric over the tacked panel and turn the four sides under. Tack it to the seat along the edge of the panel, mitering the corners as you come to them (see Figure 6). Replace the seat in the chair frame.

Decorating Bonus

The simplicity of the geometric pattern lends itself to a handsome valance (see page 115). For faster stitching on such a large project, translate the design into bargello.

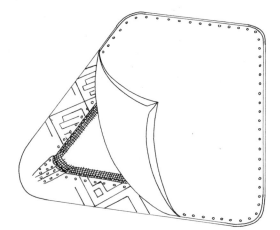

Figure 6

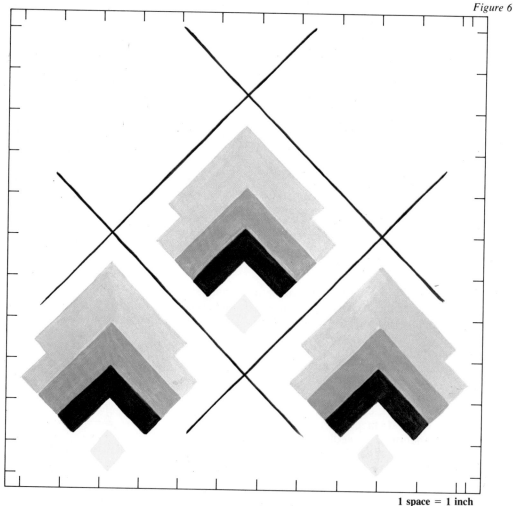

1 space = 1 inch

Bargello Director's Chair

Director's chairs seem to have almost universal appeal, perhaps because of their informality and appropriateness in many settings. They are particularly attractive in needlepoint, but since a stitched seat and back are not strong enough alone to support the weight of a person sitting, the needlepoint must be mounted over the chair's original canvas. These particular pieces are sized for a commonly available director's chair that has a 7- by 28-inch back panel and a 15½- by 18½-inch seat panel.

To cover the bargello director's chair, you will be using the following basic procedures, which have been described in detail in Section I:

- Preparing canvas
- Transferring designs to canvas
- Stitching designs
- Blocking
- Protecting edges

Stitch

Bargello pattern shown in the color guide

Canvas

No. 12 mono
Cut one piece 11 by 32 inches and another piece 20 by 23 inches. Bind the edges with masking tape.

Yarn

You will need three 32-inch threads of Persian wool for each repeat shown in the color guide.

Enlarging and Transferring

With an indelible marker, trace the outline of the back and seat panels onto each canvas. Center the pattern on each canvas and fill the area within the outline with repeat design (see Figure 1).

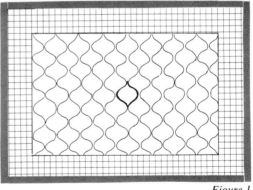

Figure 1

Special Tips for Work

Around the edges, extend the design one extra row, ending the bargello pattern as shown in Figure 2.

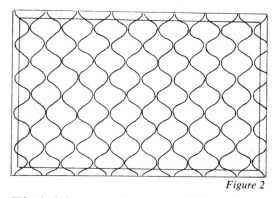

Figure 2

Finishing and Assembling

Block the needlepoint if necessary.

Around each piece, sew a row of machine stitching on the excess canvas just outside the needlepoint.

Cut the excess canvas away on all sides to within 1½ inches of the needlepoint, and cut the corners diagonally to within ½ inch of the stitching.

Miter the corners of both pieces. Tack the excess canvas to the back of the needlepoint, making sure that the rows of stitching are straight and that no unstitched canvas shows along the edges (see Figure 56).

Place the needlepoint seat panel so that it fits tightly between the two armrests and then pin it temporarily to the seat canvas. Across the front edge, whip the needlepoint to the canvas seat, hiding the stitches in the needlepoint (see Figure 3). Anchor the seat

across the back in the same way. To secure the sides, swing the armrests out of the way and blindstitch the needlepoint to the chair canvas (see Figure 4).

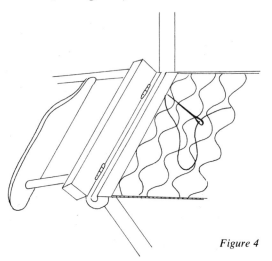

Figure 4

Center the needlepoint back panel on the canvas back of the chair and temporarily pin it in place. Across the top edge, whip the needlepoint to the canvas back, continuing around the chair posts to the rear (see Figure 5). Anchor the bottom edge of the back panel in the same way. At the rear, blindstitch the short ends to the canvas to provide a neatly finished rear view (see Figure 6).

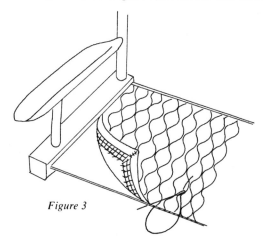

Figure 3

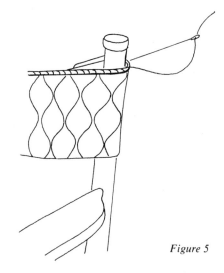

Figure 5

Figure 6

Adjusting the Design Area

If you want to alter the dimensions of this design, make a custom pattern of your chair, trace its outline on canvas, and work the bargello pattern to fill.

Decorating Bonus

Stitch a small footstool for the director's chair, reversing the shading so that the outline of each repeat will be light and the center dark.

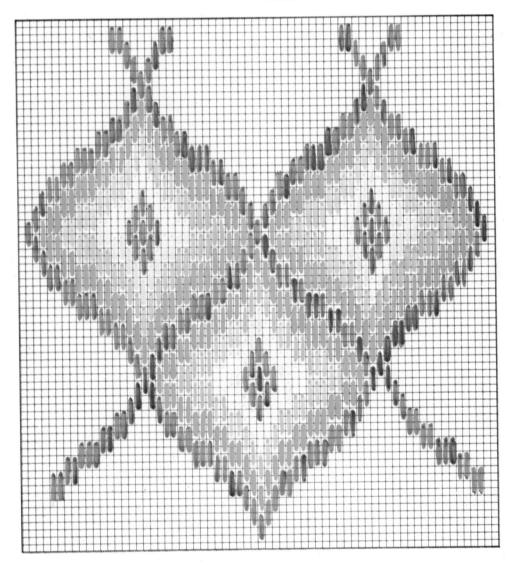

Paisley Rocking-Chair Pad

The charm of an Early American rocker and the earthy tones of this paisley chair pad make an appealing combination.

To make this rocking-chair pad, you will be using the following basic procedures, which have been described in detail in Section I:

- Preparing canvas
- Enlarging designs
- Transferring designs to canvas
- Stitching designs
- Blocking
- Protecting edges
- Welting
- Making inner pillows

Stitch

Basketweave

Canvas

No. 12 mono

Cut one piece of canvas to measure 24 by 22 inches, and bind the cut edges with masking tape.

Yarn

You will need about 8½ ounces of Persian wool.

Additional Materials

fabric backing, ½ inch larger all around than the finished needlepoint
welting, 1 inch longer than the perimeter of the finished needlepoint (about 70 inches)
thin inner pad, to fit

Enlarging and Transferring

Enlarge the design so that the depth at the center is 18 inches; the width will be about 14 inches across the back and 20½ inches across the front. Center the enlarged design under the canvas and, with an indelible marker, trace it onto the canvas.

Special Tips for Work

Around all four edges, extend the design two additional rows to provide for a seam allowance.

Finishing and Assembling

Block the needlepoint.

Sew a row of machine stitching on the excess canvas just outside the needlepoint.

Lay the needlepoint face up. Starting at the back, place the welting over it so that its unfinished edge is pointed out toward the taped canvas and the seam of the welting is directly over the needlepoint seam allowance. Baste and then sew them together on top of the welting seam, notching the welting strip at the corners (see Figure 73). When the welting is attached all around, join its ends and seam it to the needlepoint (see Figure 76).

Place the welted needlepoint and the backing fabric right sides together. Baste and then sew over the welting seam (see Figure 77). Leave an 8-inch opening in the back seam.

Trim the unstitched canvas to within ½ inch of the needlepoint; cut the corners diagonally. Turn the pad right side out, stuff it with the inner pillow, and blindstitch the opening.

Adjusting the Design Area

If the dimensions given above are not those of your chair, enlarge the design to accommodate the largest dimensions of your seat and use that portion of the enlarged design that falls within the seat outline (see Figure 1). If the shape of your particular project is different, repeat portions of the paisley pattern as needed (see Figure 2).

Decorating Bonus

Repeat some portion of the paisley pattern for a companion project such as a small headrest measuring about 10 by 4 inches (see Figure 3). Welt and stuff the headrest in the same way that you did the rocker pad.

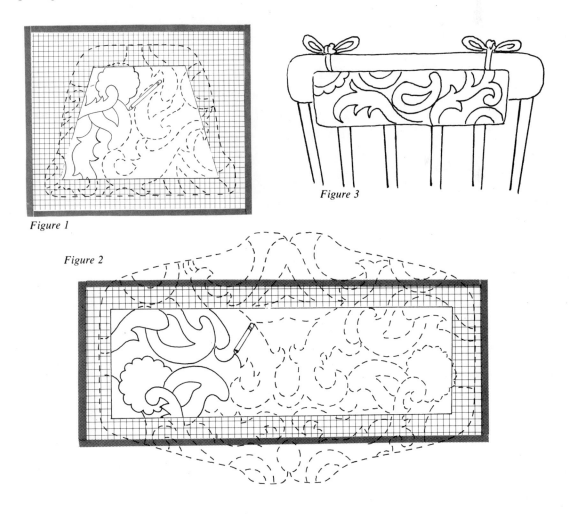

Figure 1

Figure 3

Figure 2

1 space = 1 inch

Bargello Child's-Chair Cushion

What nicer way to make a child feel special than to provide him with a childsize chair and cushion? And when the chair outlives its function, set it by the hearth to convey its own nostalgic charm. This flame-type bargello pad is 12½ inches across the front, 11 inches across the back, and 10 inches deep. It ties with corded tassels to an Early American school chair.

To make this child's-chair cushion, you will be using the following basic procedures, which have been described in detail in Section I:

- Preparing canvas
- Making custom patterns
- Transferring designs to canvas
- Stitching designs
- Blocking
- Protecting edges
- Welting
- Making inner pillows
- Making tassels

Stitch

Bargello pattern shown in the color guide

Canvas

No. 16 mono

Cut one piece so that it is 2 inches larger all around than your custom pattern, and bind the edges with masking tape.

Yarn

You will need about eleven 32-inch threads of Persian wool for each repeat shown in the color guide.

Additional Materials

fabric backing, ½ inch larger all around than the finished needlepoint
welting, 1 inch longer than the perimeter of the finished needlepoint (about 43 inches)

2 pieces of fine silk cording, each 26 inches long
4 yarn tassels
inner pillow to fit

Enlarging and Transferring

Make a custom pattern of your chair seat and, using an indelible marker, trace it onto the canvas. Center the bargello pattern on the canvas both horizontally and vertically and work it to fill the area within the outline (see Figure 1).

Special Tips for Work

Around all four edges, extend the design

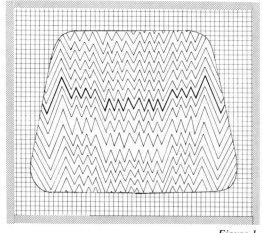

Figure 1

two extra rows to provide for a seam allowance.

End the bargello design at the edges, as shown in Figure 2.

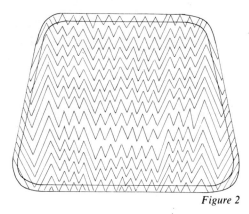

Figure 2

Finishing and Assembling

Block the needlepoint.

Sew a row of machine stitching on the excess canvas just outside the needlepoint.

Lay the needlepoint face up. Starting at the back, place the welting over it so that its unfinished edge is pointed out toward the taped canvas edge and the seam of the welting is directly over the needlepoint seam allowance. Baste and then sew them together on top of the welting seam, notching the welting strip at the corners (see Figure 73). When the welting is attached all around, join

its ends and seam it to the needlepoint (See Figure 76).

Lay the fabric backing face up. Fold the lengths of cording in half and pin one over each of the two rear corners of the backing, loose ends facing in and loop extending out about 1 inch. Lay the welted needlepoint over the backing, face down. Baste and then sew them together over the welting seam, starting at a rear corner (see Figure 3). Stitch over the cording ties as you come to them, and stop right after you have turned the last corner so that most of the back seam is still open.

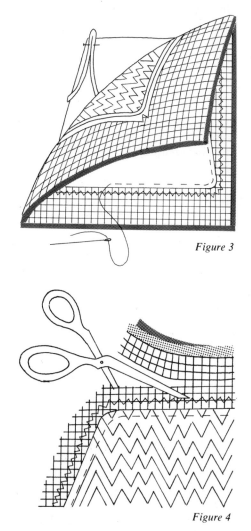

Figure 3

Figure 4

Trim the unstitched canvas edges and the backing fabric to within ½ inch of the needlepoint, and cut the corners diagonally (see Figure 4).

Turn right side out, insert the inner pillow, and blindstitch the opening. Sew a tassel to each end of the cording and tie around the chair back.

Decorating Bonus

If you are lucky enough to have a window seat in your home, turn it into a very special hideaway corner for your child by cushioning it with a box pillow done in the same pattern as the chair; use the same or contrasting colors.

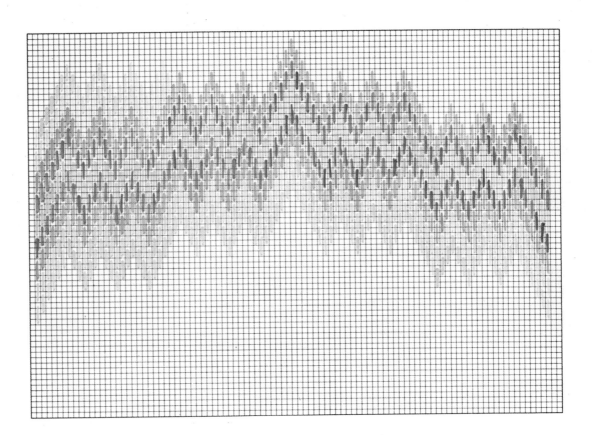

Bargello Hall-Bench Pad

The undulating lines of this bargello pattern look like a collection of seashells neatly lined up on a charming early English spindle bench. The thick cushion, which measures 1½ by 18 by 39 inches, is boxed, welted, backed with wide-wale corduroy, and shaped at the back to accommodate the corner spindles.

To make this bench pad, you will use the following basic procedures, which are described in detail in Section I:
- Preparing canvas
- Making custom patterns
- Transferring designs to canvas
- Stitching designs
- Blocking canvas
- Protecting edges
- Welting
- Making boxing strips
- Making inner pillows

Stitch

Bargello pattern shown in the color guide on page 62

Canvas

No. 12 mono
   Cut one piece so that it is 2 inches larger all around than your custom pattern and bind the edges with masking tape.

Yarn

You will need about eight 32-inch threads of Persian wool to stitch the full repeat shown in the color guide.

Additional Materials

fabric backing, ½ inch larger all around than the finished needlepoint
boxing strip, 3½ inches wide and 1 inch longer than the perimeter of the seat cushion
2 strips of welting, each the length of the boxing strip
slab of foam rubber, 2½ inches thick and the size of the finished needlepoint

Enlarging and Transferring

Make a custom pattern of your bench seat, and trace it onto canvas with an indelible marker. Center the bargello pattern on the canvas and work it to fill the area within the outline (see Figure 1).

Special Tips for Work

Around all edges, extend the design two extra rows to provide for a seam allowance.

At the edges, end the design as shown in Figure 2.

Finishing and Assembling

Block the needlepoint if necessary.

Sew a row of machine stitching on the excess canvas just outside the needlepoint.

Lay the needlepoint face up. Starting in the middle of the back edge, place the welting over it so that its unfinished edge is pointed out toward the taped canvas edge and the seam of the welting is directly over the needlepoint seam allowance. Baste and then sew them together on top of the welting seam, notching the welting strip at the corners (see Figure 73). When the welting is attached all around, join its ends and seam it to the needlepoint (see Figure 76).

With the fabric backing face up, sew the second welting strip to it in the same way,

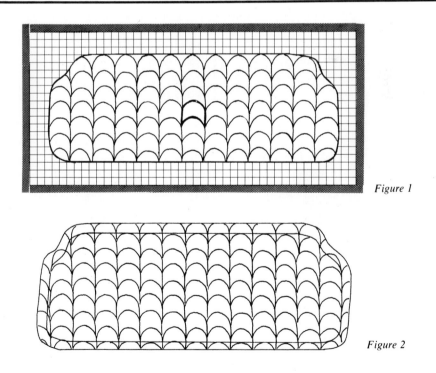

Figure 1

Figure 2

leaving a ½-inch seam allowance all around the backing.

Lay the needlepoint face up. Starting in the middle of the back edge, place the boxing strip face down so that its seam allowance lies directly over the seam of the welting. Baste and then sew the boxing strip to the welted needlepoint around the four sides, notching the corners. When you reach your starting point, join the two ends. Trim the unstitched canvas edges to within ½ inch of the needlepoint and cut the corners diagonally (see Figure 92).

Lay the welted fabric backing face up and, with the welted boxed needlepoint still inside out, sew the boxing strip to the welted backing, as described above. Start at one rear corner and stop just after you have turned the fourth corner so that most of the back seam is open. Turn right side out, fill with the foam rubber slab, and blindstitch the opening (see Figure 3).

Decorating Bonus

Stitch a giant floor pillow in this pattern; the bargello will cover the canvas quickly.

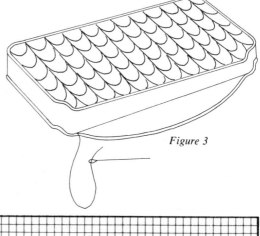

Figure 3

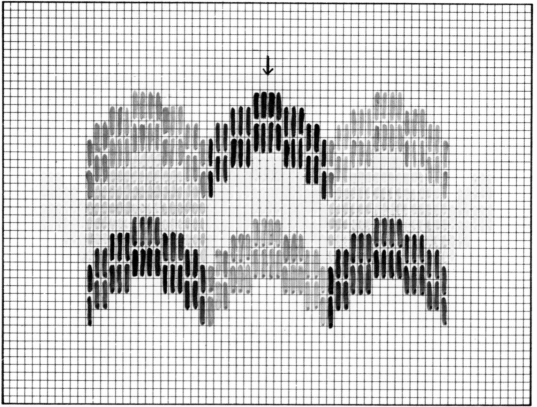

Art Deco Bench Cushion

The narrow, graceful proportions of an antique English mahogany bench contrast engagingly with this trim cushion, the design of which is in the currently popular Art Deco style. The colors were borrowed from a nearby contemporary painting.

To make the bench cushion, you will use the following basic procedures, which are described in detail in Section I:

- Preparing canvas
- Enlarging designs
- Transferring designs to canvas
- Stitching designs
- Blocking
- Protecting edges
- Welting
- Making boxing strips
- Making inner pillows

Stitch

Basketweave

Canvas

No. 12 mono

Cut one piece 13 by 38 inches, and bind the edges with masking tape.

Yarn

You will need about 7½ ounces of Persian wool.

Additional Materials

fabric backing, ½ inch larger all around than the finished needlepoint

boxing strip, 2 inches wide and 1 inch longer than the perimeter of the cushion (about 86 inches)

2 strips of welting, each the length of the boxing strip

slab of foam rubber, 1 inch thick and the size of the finished needlepoint

Enlarging and Transferring

Enlarge the design so that the width measures 34 inches; the depth will be about 8½ inches. Center the enlarged design face up under the canvas and, using an indelible marker, trace it onto the canvas.

Special Tips for Work

Around all edges, extend the design two extra rows to provide for a seam allowance.

Finishing and Assembling

Block the needlepoint.

Sew a row of machine stitching on the excess canvas just outside the needlepoint.

Lay the needlepoint face up. Starting in the middle of the back edge, place the welting over it so that its unfinished edge is pointed out toward the taped canvas and the seam of the welting is directly over the needlepoint seam allowance. Baste and then sew them together on top of the welting seam, notching the welting strip at the corners (see Figure 73). When the welting is attached all around, join its ends and seam it to the needlepoint (see Figure 76).

With the fabric backing face up, sew the second welting strip to it in the same way, leaving a ½-inch seam allowance all around the backing.

Lay the needlepoint face up. Starting at the middle of the back edge, place the boxing strip face down so that its seam allowance lies directly over the seam of the welting. Baste and then sew the boxing strip to the welted needlepoint around the four sides, notching the corners. When you reach your starting point, join the two ends. Trim the unstitched canvas edges to within ½ inch of the needlepoint and cut the corners diagonally (see Figure 92).

Lay the welted fabric backing face up and, with the welted boxed needlepoint still inside out, sew the boxing strip to the welted backing, as described above. Start at one back corner and stop just after you have turned the last corner so that most of the back seam is open. Turn right side out, fill with foam rubber; blindstitch opening.

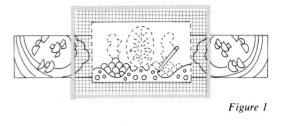

Figure 1

Adjusting the Design Area

If your own bench is a wider rectangle than the one shown, enlarge either the center section (see Figure 1) or a side section (see Figure 2) to fill your dimensions.

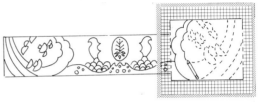

Figure 2

Decorating Bonus

Hang your own print or painting over the bench and, using the same Art Deco design, change the colors to reflect those in the work of art.

1 space = 1 inch

Flowered-Plaid Vanity Seat

Design derived from fabric and wall covering by Hannett Morrow Fischer, Inc., New York.

A prettily padded bench can lead many lives in a bedroom/sitting room—use it in front of a vanity table, at the foot of a bed to hold the spread at night, as an extra pull-up seat. This slightly contoured bench is upholstered with a simple plaid design that incorporates four different flowers taken from a wallpaper pattern. The bench is 20½ by 27 inches overall, including the allowance for the padding. The design can easily be adapted to fit any size seat.

To upholster the padded floral vanity bench, you will use the following basic procedures, which are described in detail in Section I:
- Preparing canvas
- Enlarging designs
- Transferring designs to canvas
- Stitching designs
- Blocking
- Protecting edges
- Cording

Stitch

Basketweave

Canvas

No. 12 mono
Cut one piece 25 by 31 inches, and bind the edges with masking tape.

Yarn

You will need about 3 ounces of Persian wool for each four-square repeat in Figure 1.

Additional Materials

cambric for lining, ½ inch larger all around than the bottom of the seat.
cording, twice the perimeter of the finished needlepoint

Enlarging and Transferring

With an indelible marker, trace the outline of the bench, including the allowance for the height of the padding, onto the canvas.

Enlarge the design so that the height measures 10 inches; the width will be about 10¾ inches. Place the enlarged design face up under the canvas and, using an indelible marker, trace it onto the canvas. Move the design to adjacent sections of the canvas and make additional tracings until the outline is filled (see Figure 1).

Special Tips for Work

On all four sides, extend the design 1 extra inch.

For accuracy, you can plot the plaid on graph paper before stitching it.

Finishing and Assembling

Block the needlepoint.

Sew a row of machine stitching on the excess canvas just outside the needlepoint.

On all four sides, cut the excess canvas away to within 1½ inches of the needlepoint; cut the corners diagonally to within 1 inch of the needlepoint.

Figure 1

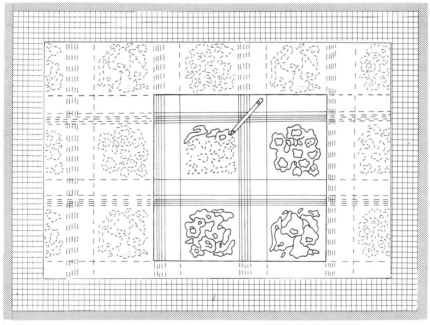

68

Remove the existing cambric and upholstery from the bench, and replace the padding if necessary.

Place the needlepoint face down on work surface. Center the padded bench upside down over needlepoint and temporarily tack needlepoint loosely to the sides and the ends.

To upholster around one of the legs, turn one corner of needlepoint up around it. Starting at the corner point, cut a slit toward the leg, stopping just short of it (see Figure

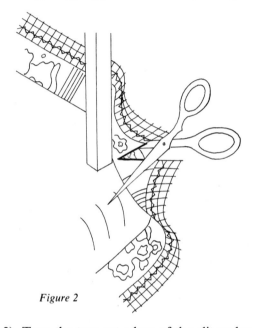

Figure 2

2). Turn the two cut edges of the slit under, and tack each edge to the underside of the bench, pulling each taut around the leg (see

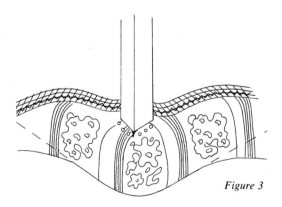

Figure 3

Figure 3). Anchor the needlepoint around the leg with upholstery tacks.

Upholster around the other legs in the same way.

Remove the temporary tacks from the long contoured back edge, and tack the needlepoint to the underside of the bench, pulling the needlepoint taut. Tack the front contoured edge in the same manner, pulling the needlepoint smooth but not so taut that you lose the contour (see Figure 4). Repeat tacking procedure for remaining two sides.

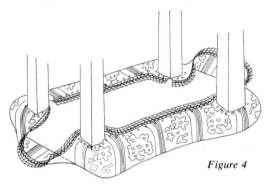

Figure 4

Turn the bench over and tack any loose edges to the frame. Lay the cambric over the underside of the seat, and turn the four sides under so that they just cover the needlepoint tacks. Tack the cambric to the frame, pulling the lining taut and mitering the corners as you come to them (see Figure 5).

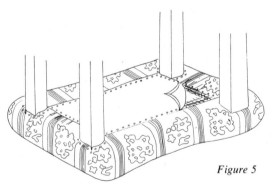

Figure 5

If you wish to have a trim finish, you can blindstitch a double row of cording around the bottom edge of the padded side of the seat (see Figure 6).

Adjusting the Design Area

If your own bench is a different size from this one, make a custom pattern for it, outline it on canvas, and trace the enlarged design to fill it, as described above.

Decorating Bonus

Make each of the four flowers in the design into a throw pillow for the bed, or combine them into one large "bouquet" pillow.

Figure 6

1 space = 1 inch

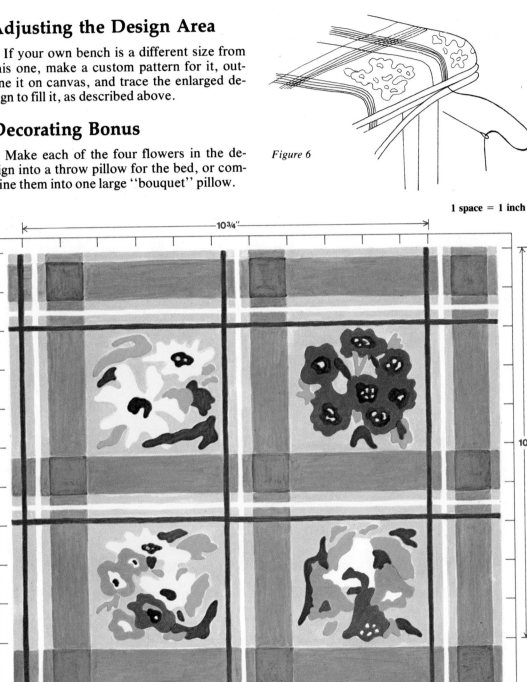

10¾"

10"

Country French Footstool Pad

The unexpected juxtaposition of different periods and styles can be surprisingly delightful, as you can see in this charming footstool, which weds a French Provincial floral print to a contemporary Lucite base (see "Sources").

To make this footstool pad, you will use the following basic procedures, which are described in detail in Section I:

- Preparing canvas
- Enlarging designs
- Transferring designs to canvas
- Stitching designs
- Blocking
- Protecting edges
- Welting
- Making boxing strips
- Making inner pillows

Stitch

Basketweave

Canvas

No. 12 mono

Cut one piece 13 by 16 inches, and bind the edges with masking tape.

Yarn

You will need about 3 ounces of Persian wool; 2 ounces of it will be used for the background.

Additional Materials

fabric backing, ½ inch larger all around than the finished needlepoint

boxing strip, 2½ inches wide and 1 inch longer than the perimeter of the pad (about 43 inches)

2 strips of welting, each the length of the boxing strip

slab of foam rubber, 1½ inches thick and the size of the finished needlepoint

2 strips of Velcro, each 8 inches long

Enlarging and Transferring

Enlarge the design so that the width measures 9 inches; the length will be about 12 inches. Center the enlarged design face up under the canvas and, using an indelible marker, trace it onto the canvas.

Special Tips for Work

Around all four edges, extend the design two extra rows to provide for a seam allowance.

Finishing and Assembling

Block the needlepoint.

Sew a row of machine stitching on the excess canvas just outside the needlepoint.

Lay the needlepoint face up. Starting in the middle of the back edge, place the welting over it so that its unfinished edge is pointed out toward the taped canvas and the seam of the welting is directly over the needlepoint seam allowance. Baste and then sew them together on top of the welting seam (see Figure 73), notching the welting strip at the corners. When the welting is attached all around, join its ends and seam it to the needlepoint (see Figure 76).

With the fabric backing face up, sew the second welting strip to it in the same way, leaving a ½-inch seam allowance all around the backing.

Lay the needlepoint face up. Starting at the middle of the back edge, place the boxing strip face down so that its seam allowance lies directly over the seam of the welting. Baste and then sew the boxing strip to the welted needlepoint around the four sides, notching the corners. When you reach your starting point, join the two ends. Trim the unstitched canvas edges to within ½ inch of the needlepoint and cut the corners diagonally (see Figure 92).

Lay the welted fabric backing face up and, with the welted boxed needlepoint still inside out, sew the boxing strip to the welted backing, as described above. Start at one side of the back and stop just after you have turned the last corner so that most of the back seam is open. Turn right side out, fill with the foam rubber slab, and blindstitch the opening.

At each short edge, anchor the cushion to the footstool with Velcro; blindstitch one side of the strip to the fabric backing and glue its mate to the footstool (see Figure 1).

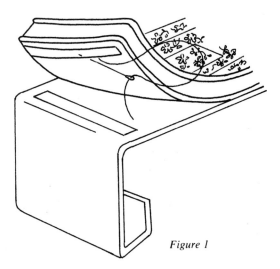

Figure 1

72

Adjusting the Design Area

The design can be enlarged as many times as you need, but the nature of the pattern does not permit any change in its proportions.

Decorating Bonus

Instead of using a solid color for the backing fabric, look for a small two-color pattern that picks up two closely related colors in the needlepoint.

1 space = 1 inch

Chapter 2

Pillows

Four coordinated pillows—Tulip Trio, Ombré Rose, Persian Patchwork, and Candy-Striped Floral.

Needlepoint pillows are deservedly popular—they are the quickest and easiest way to introduce a brand new look to a room. A few pillows of different shapes and designs will transform even the sparest sofa into a profusion of pattern and color; one splendid pillow can brighten a hitherto nondescript chair. But simply piling pattern on pattern does have its risks if there is no plan to the abundance.

The following four pillows—all different shapes and designs—are interrelated and planned as a grouping. The square pillow is a patchwork of Persian motifs from which flow the designs of all the others. The three "siblings" develop design details or colors found in the patchwork, using them in different formations. The grouping as a whole has a unity, yet great diversity within it. Make the whole set or choose individuals.

All the pillows are backed with velvet in colors taken from the master pillow. The square and rectangular ones are knife-edged and welted; the round one is boxed and welted; the shaped rose is knife-edged but not welted.

Persian Patchwork

To make this patchwork pillow, you will be using the following basic procedures, which have been described in detail in Section I:

- Preparing canvas
- Enlarging designs
- Transferring designs to canvas
- Stitching designs
- Blocking
- Protecting edges
- Welting
- Making inner pillows

Stitch

Basketweave

Canvas

No. 12 mono

Cut one piece 18 inches square, and bind the edges with masking tape.

Yarn

You will need about 6 ounces of Persian wool.

Additional Materials

fabric backing, ½ inch larger all around than the finished needlepoint

welting, 1 inch longer than the perimeter of the finished needlepoint (about 57 inches)

inner pillow to fit

Enlarging and Transferring

Enlarge the design so that it measures 14 inches square. Center it under the canvas and, using an indelible marker, trace it onto the canvas.

Special Tips for Work

Around all edges, extend the design two extra rows to provide for a seam allowance.

Finishing and Assembling

Block the needlepoint.

Sew a row of machine stitching on the excess canvas just outside the needlepoint.

Lay the needlepoint face up. Starting at the bottom, place the welting over it so that the unfinished edge is pointed out toward the taped canvas and the seam of the welting is directly over the needlepoint seam allowance. Baste and then sew them together on top of the welting seam, notching the welting strip at the corners (see Figure 73). When the welting is attached all around, join its ends and seam it to the needlepoint (see Figure 76).

Place the welted needlepoint and the backing fabric right sides together. Baste and then sew over the welting seam (see Figure 77), leaving an 8-inch opening in the bottom seam.

Trim the unstitched canvas to within ½ inch of the needlepoint, and cut the corners diagonally (see Figure 1). Turn right side out, stuff with the inner pillow, and blind-stitch the opening.

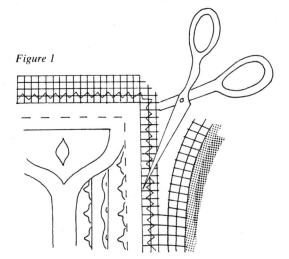

Figure 1

1 space = 1 inch

Candy-Striped Floral

To make this pillow, you will use the following basic procedures, which are described in detail in Section I:
- Preparing canvas
- Enlarging designs
- Transferring designs to canvas
- Stitching designs
- Blocking
- Protecting edges
- Welting
- Making inner pillows

Stitch

Basketweave

Canvas

No. 10 mono
 Cut one piece 16 by 20 inches, and bind the edges with masking tape.

Yarn

 You will need about 6 ounces of Persian wool; more than 2 ounces of it will be used for the background.

Additional Materials

fabric backing, ½ inch larger all around than the finished needlepoint
welting, 1 inch longer than perimeter of finished needlepoint (about 57 inches)
inner pillow to fit

Enlarging and Transferring

 Enlarge the design so that it measures 12 inches wide; it will be about 16 inches long. Center under the canvas and, using an indelible marker, trace it onto the canvas.

Special Tips for Work

 Around all edges, extend design two extra rows to provide for a seam allowance.

Finishing and Assembling

 Block the needlepoint.
 Sew a row of machine stitching on the excess canvas just outside the needlepoint.
 Lay the needlepoint face up. Starting in the middle of one side, place the welting over it so that the unfinished edge is pointed out toward the taped canvas and the seam of the welting is directly over the needlepoint seam allowance. Baste and then sew on top of the welting seam, notching the welting strip at the corners (See Figure 73). When the welting is attached all around, join its ends and seam it to the needlepoint (see Figure 76).
 Place the welted needlepoint and the backing fabric right sides together. Baste and then sew over the welting seam (see Figure 77), leaving an 8-inch opening in the middle of one seam.
 Trim the unstitched canvas to within ½ inch of the needlepoint and cut the corners diagonally (see Figure 1). Turn right side out, insert the inner pillow, and blindstitch the opening.

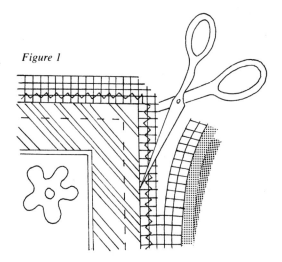

Figure 1

1 space = 1 inch

Tulip Trio

To make this pillow, you will use the following basic procedures, which are described in detail in Section I:
- Preparing canvas
- Enlarging designs
- Transferring designs to canvas
- Stitching designs
- Blocking
- Protecting edges
- Welting
- Making boxing strips
- Making inner pillows

Stitch

Basketweave

Canvas

No. 10 mono
Cut one piece 18 inches square, and bind the edges with masking tape.

Yarn

You will need about 4½ ounces of Persian wool; 3 ounces of it will be used for the background.

Additional Materials

fabric backing, ½ inch larger all around than the finished needlepoint
boxing strip, 3 inches wide and 1 inch longer than the circumference of the pillow (about 44 inches)
2 strips of welting, each the length of the boxing strip
inner pillow to fit

Enlarging and Transferring

Enlarge the design so that it measures 14 inches in diameter. Center it under the canvas and, using an indelible marker, trace it onto the canvas.

Special Tips for Work

Around the circumference, extend the design two extra rows to provide for a seam allowance.

Finishing and Assembling

Block the needlepoint.

Sew a row of machine stitching on the excess canvas just outside the needlepoint.

Lay the needlepoint face up. Starting at the bottom, place the welting over it so that the unfinished edge is pointed out toward the taped canvas and the seam of the welting is directly over the needlepoint seam allowance. Baste and then sew on top of the welting seam, notching the welting strip occasionally to accommodate the curve (see Figure 1). When the welting is attached all

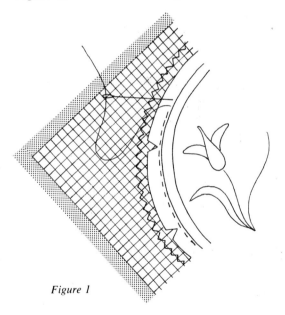

Figure 1

around, join its ends and seam it to the needlepoint (see Figure 2).

With the fabric backing face up, sew the second welting strip to it in the same way as

80

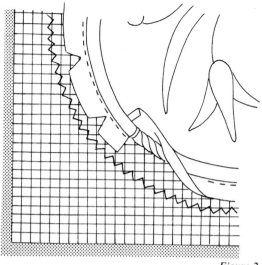

Figure 2

you reach the starting point, join the two ends. Trim the unstitched canvas to within ½ inch of the needlepoint (see Figure 3).

Lay the welted fabric backing face up. With the welted boxed needlepoint still inside out, sew the boxing strip to the welted backing, as described above. Leave an opening in the bottom seam that is about 8 inches long (see Figure 4). Turn right side out, insert inner pillow, and blindstitch the opening (see Figure 5).

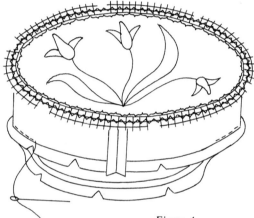

described above, leaving a ½-inch seam allowance all around the backing.

Lay the needlepoint face up. Starting at the bottom, place the boxing strip face down so that its seam allowance lies directly over the seam of the welting. Baste and then sew the boxing strip to the welted needlepoint around the circumference, notching it occasionally to accommodate the curve. When

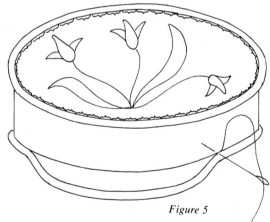

Figure 4

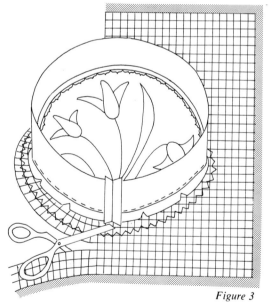

Figure 3

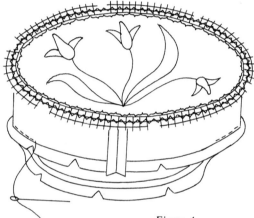

Figure 5

1 space = 1 inch

1 space = 1 inch

Ombré Rose

To make this ombré rose pillow, you will be using the following basic procedures, which have been described in detail in Section I:

- Preparing canvas
- Enlarging designs
- Transferring designs to canvas
- Stitching designs
- Blocking
- Protecting edges
- Making inner pillows

Stitch

Basketweave

Canvas

Use No. 12 mono
Cut one piece 12 by 13 inches, and bind the edges with masking tape.

Yarn

You will need about 2 ounces of Persian wool.

Additional Materials

fabric backing, ½ inch larger all around than finished needlepoint
inner pillow to fit

Enlarging and Transferring

Enlarge the design so that it is 9 inches across its widest part; the height will be about 7 inches. Center the enlarged design face up under the canvas and, using an indelible marker, trace it onto the canvas.

Special Tips for Work

To give the rose shading and depth, work from light to dark by combining yarn strands of the closest shades into each working thread (see page 24). This will provide for a continuous change of color without sharp breaks.

Around all sides, extend the design for two extra rows to provide for a seam allowance.

Finishing and Assembling

Block the needlepoint.

Sew a row of machine stitching on the excess canvas just outside the needlepoint.

Place the needlepoint and backing fabric right sides together. Baste and then sew just inside the needlepoint seam allowance, following the shape of the pillow (see Figure 1). Leave an 8-inch opening in the bottom seam.

Trim unstitched canvas and excess backing to within ½ inch of needlepoint. Turn inside out, insert inner pillow, and blindstitch opening (see Figure 2).

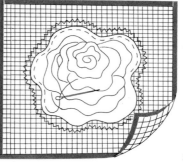

Figure 1

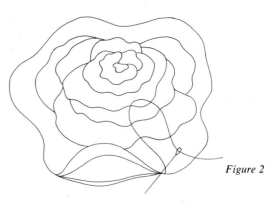

Figure 2

Turkoman

Nothing could be nicer than to have a ready-to-use pillow the minute you make your last needlepoint stitch, which is the happy result when you work a prefinished pillow. You buy it already backed and welted—in a variety of colors, sizes, and fabrics, and fitted with a plain needlepoint panel that is usually of No. 12 interlocking canvas. Just zip the canvas face off the fabric back, transfer a favorite design onto it, and get to work.

This particular Oriental design has been adapted from a Turkoman tribal *gul*, or insignia, and is finished as a 12-inch-square box pillow in cotton suede cloth (see "Sources").

To make this pillow, you will use the following basic procedures, which are described in detail in Section I:

- Transferring designs to canvas
- Stitching designs
- Blocking
- Making inner pillows

Stitch

Basketweave

Canvas

No. 12 interlocking

Yarn

You will need about 4 ounces of Persian wool.

Additional Materials

inner pillow to fit

Enlarging and Transferring

Mark the center of the canvas. Following the graph in Figure 1, which is the top right quarter of the design, work out from the center point.

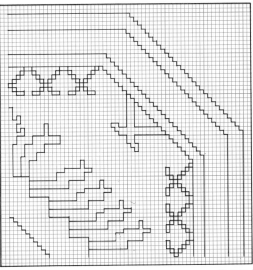

Figure 1

Special Tips for Work

Starting at the center point, stitch one quarter of the design; then use that as the model for the rest of the pillow. The other three quarters repeat the same motifs in reverse, or "flopped," and should be worked to match (see Figure 2).

Work right up to the fabric edge, even tucking stitches under the welting.

Finishing and Assembling

Block the welted needlepoint. Use rust-proof tacks and insert them carefully just inside the welting, taking care not to split any stitches (see Figure 3).

Pack the inner pillow into the backing half and zip the needlepoint top into place (see Figure 4).

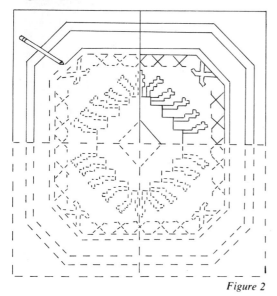

Figure 2

Decorating Bonus

Make a companion pillow in a simple geometric pattern like that of the letter tray on page 169, which uses the colors of the Oriental design.

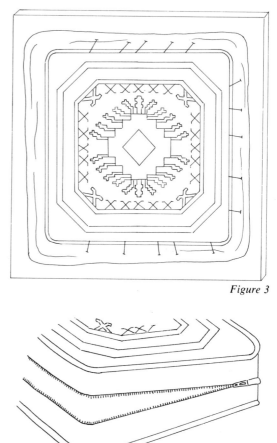

Figure 3

Figure 4

Chapter 3

Tables

Patchwork Parson's Table

Design derived from the fabric design "Vivolino," sold exclusively at Clarence House, New York, to the trade. Chair (also shown on cover) supplied by Walters Wicker Wonderland, New York.

An upholstered table provides a sophisticated accent in a formal living room, and parson's tables, with their clean, straight lines, are especially suitable for covering. This particular parson's table is 16 inches square and 16 inches high. It is an all-plastic model, is reasonable in cost, and is readily available in many furniture and department stores. If you have a parson's table of different dimensions, see "Adjusting the Design Area" below and follow the instructions.

To cover the patchwork parson's table, you will be using the following basic procedures, described in detail in Section I:
- Preparing canvas
- Enlarging designs
- Transferring designs to canvas
- Stitching designs
- Joining
- Blocking
- Protecting edges
- Lacing
- Lining

Stitches

Basketweave
Overcasting on legs

Canvas

No. 12 mono

Cut one piece measuring 20 inches square for the tabletop and another piece measuring 20 by 60 inches for the legs. Bind the edges with masking tape.

Yarn

You will need about 25 ounces of Persian wool.

Additional Materials

fabric for lining underside of table

Enlarging and Transferring

Enlarge the design for the tabletop so that it is exactly 16 inches square. Enlarge the design for the table legs so that the height is 16 inches; the width will be about 64 inches. Center the enlarged tabletop design face up under the canvas square and, using an indelible marker, trace the design onto the canvas. In the same way, trace the design for the legs of the table onto the 20 by 60-inch rectangular canvas.

Special Tips for Work

Around all four edges of the top section canvas, extend the design two extra rows to provide for a seam allowance. You will need this seam allowance in order to join the tabletop canvas to the leg canvas.

Along the top and each side of the leg canvas—that is, AC, AB, and CD in Figure 1—extend the design two extra rows to provide for a seam allowance.

Finishing and Assembling

Block the needlepoint.

Along all four edges of both pieces, sew a row of machine stitching just outside the needlepoint.

Attach the rectangular leg section to the square top section as follows: Lay the top piece face up and the leg section over it face down so that right sides are together. Place the long edge with the seam allowance (AC in Figure 1) over any one of the four sides of the top section, making sure to match the seam allowances. Baste and then sew by machine or hand, stitching just inside the two extra rows of seam allowance (see Figure 2). As you come to each corner, notch the raw canvas of the leg section up to, but not including, the protective row of machine stitching (see Figure 3) so that you can turn it to fit the square top section. Sew around the top in this manner.

A   C

B   D

Figure 1

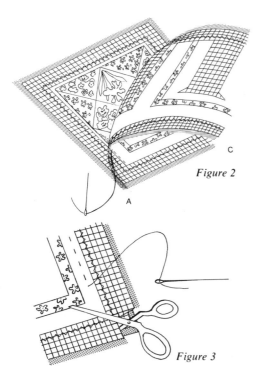

Figure 2

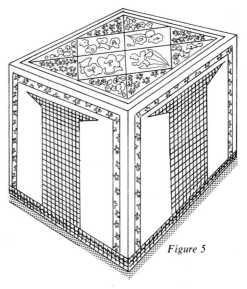

Figure 3

With the needlepoint still inside out, seam the two side edges of the leg section together (AB to CD in Figure 4). To do this, place the right sides of both edges together and seam by hand or machine just inside the two extra rows of seam allowance.

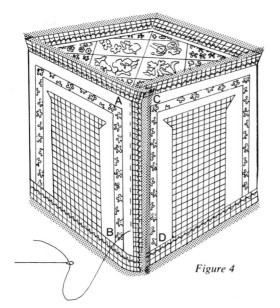

Figure 4

Cut away the excess canvas around all seamed joins up to, but not including, the protective row of machine stitching. Steam-press all seams open.

To finish the four table legs, start by turning the needlepoint "cube" right side out (see Figure 5). The following instructions are for one side. Repeat the same procedure for all four sides.

Figure 5

Sew a row of machine stitching from F to G and from J to K as closely as you can to the edge of the stitched needlepoint (see Figure 6). Cut the unstitched canvas from E to F to G and from H to J to K. Cut the canvas from L to M and discard the excess. Apply a thin line of glue along all cut edges and let dry. Turn under a 1-inch hem in the unstitched canvas at LM and secure with strong carpet thread or dental floss. Along the newly cut edges EF and HJ, fold the unstitched canvas back so that just one vertical canvas thread shows (see Figure 7). Tack the turned-back hem to the stitched needlepoint, and steam-press both hemmed edges. Work an overcasting stitch along all four cut canvas diagonals (see Figure 8) to protect the edges.

After all four sides have been done, slip the needlepoint over the parson's table and turn it upside down.

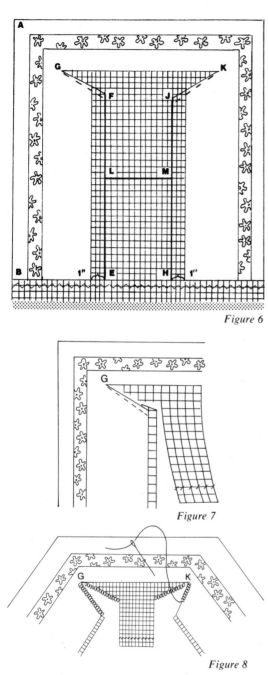

Figure 6

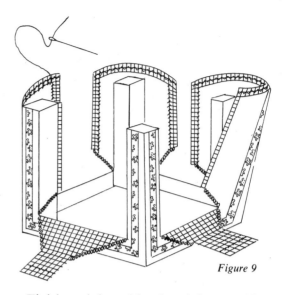

Figure 9

Finish each leg with a butt join, matching mesh carefully. To do this, start from the bottom of each leg and whip the sides together with a full triple strand of Persian yarn (see Figure 10).

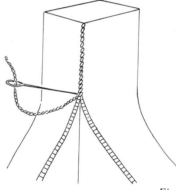

Figure 7

Figure 10

With the table still turned upside down, turn in the four unstitched canvas flaps. Pull them taut so that the tabletop and four aprons are trimly upholstered and then lace opposite sides together (see Figure 11).

Fit the lining to the underside and then turn under and blindstitch it to the edge of the canvas (see Figure 12).

Figure 8

At the bottom of each leg, cut away the excess canvas to within 1 inch of the needlepoint. Turn the canvas hem under and tack it to the inside of the stitched needlepoint (see Figure 9).

Adjusting the Design Area

If your table is rectangular rather than square, repeat some of the floral diamond patches (see Figure 13) and then adjust the widths of the borders as necessary. For the legs, simply extend or abbreviate the design to fit your table.

Decorating Bonus

Use the table design as a central focus for coordinate needlepoint: Stitch the whole top design for one throw pillow and one or more of the floral diamond patches for another; use the floral strip on the legs for window shade trim.

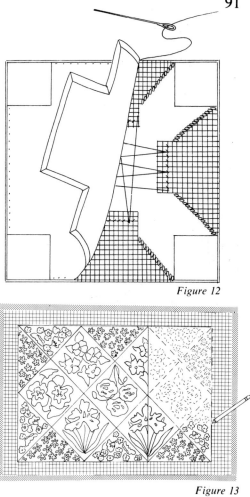

Figure 12

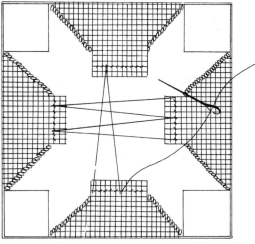

Figure 11

Figure 13

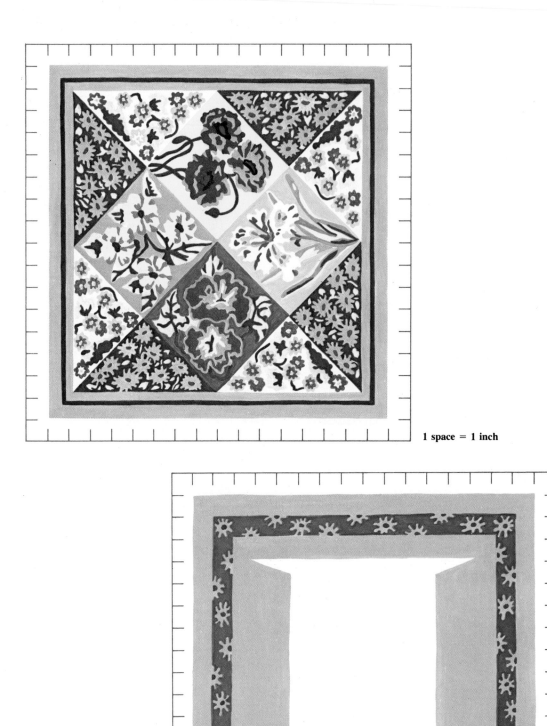

1 space = 1 inch

1 space = 1 inch

Egyptian-Motif Coffee Table

Coffee tables, often used to show off handsome books or collection treasures, can themselves become objects of admiration. This particular table, made of an antique picture frame that has been fitted with wooden legs, displays a striking design of Egyptian origin. The needlepoint is mounted like a framed picture and protected by a sheet of glass.

To make the coffee table, you will use the following basic procedures, which are described in detail in Section I:

- Preparing canvas
- Enlarging designs
- Transferring designs to canvas
- Stitching designs
- Blocking
- Mitering corners
- Lacing
- Lining

Stitch

Basketweave

Canvas

No. 10 mono
Cut one piece 20 by 26 inches, and bind the edges with masking tape.

Yarn

You will need about 13½ ounces of Persian wool; about 6 ounces of it will be used for the background.

Additional Materials

frame to accommodate the mounted needlepoint, fitted with a set of 15-inch-high legs,
 metal or wood
plywood, ¼ inch thick, measuring 20 by 22
 inches
glass sheet to fit frame
heavy brown paper for backing

Enlarging and Transferring

Enlarge the design so that the width measures 22 inches; the depth will be about 20 inches. Center it face up under the canvas and, using an indelible marker, trace it onto the canvas.

Special Tips for Work

Around all four edges, extend the design for four extra rows.

Finishing and Assembling

Block the needlepoint.

Sew a row of machine stitching on the excess canvas about ½ inch out from the needlepoint. Cut the excess canvas away on all four sides to within 1½ inches of the needlepoint, and cut the corners diagonally to within 1 inch of the needlepoint. Glue the cut edges and let dry (see Figure 1).

Lay the needlepoint face down on your work surface and center the plywood board over it, making sure that the rows of stitching are perfectly straight on all four sides. Temporarily anchor the needlepoint to the edge of the plywood board with thin tacks (see Figure 57a).

Lace opposite sides of the canvas together with heavy carpet thread, starting in the center of the sides and working to within 2 inches of each corner (see Figure 2). Miter each corner and sew the mitered seams. Finish lacing opposite sides together (see Figure 3).

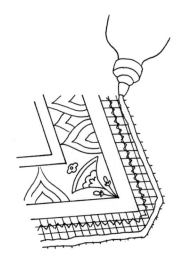

Figure 1

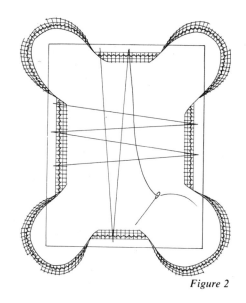

Figure 2

Clean glass well and lay it into the frame; insert the mounted panel and secure tightly with appropriate hardware or nails.

Cut a piece of heavy brown paper to fit the back of the frame and glue in place (see Figure 4).

Decorating Bonus

Pick up the border design for curtain trim or drapery ties.

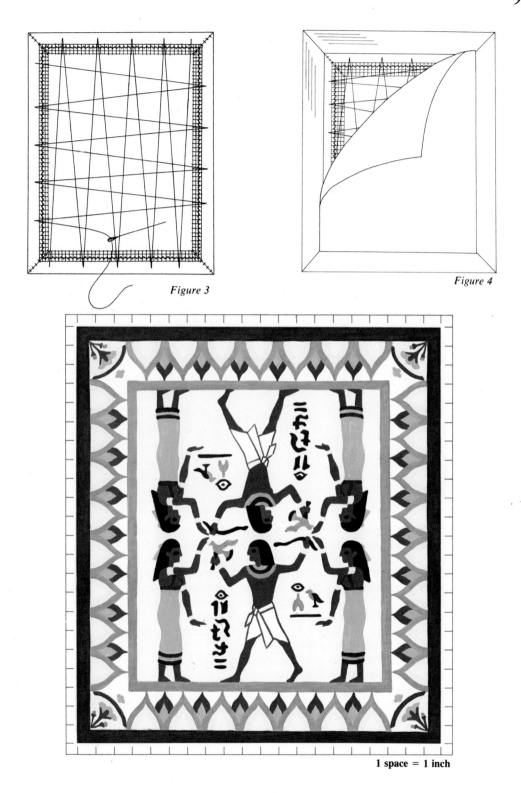

Figure 3

Figure 4

1 space = 1 inch

Kazak Card-Table Cover

You don't need to be a card buff to enjoy this Oriental design and its Kazak motifs; just drape it on any table for a splash of color. But if cards are your game, you'll appreciate this cover even more—its flat surface will ease playing, its decorative center will delight your eye, and its wide felt borders will please your hands.

The 16-inch-square needlepoint is set into a 48-inch-square piece of felt. This provides a 9-inch drop all around when used on a standard 30-inch card table. Naturally, the drop will vary in length if your table has different dimensions.

To make the Kazak card-table cover, you will be using the following basic procedures, which have been described in detail in Section I:
- Preparing canvas
- Enlarging designs
- Transferring designs to canvas
- Stitching designs
- Blocking
- Protecting edges

Stitch

Basketweave

Canvas

No. 12 mono

Cut one piece of canvas to measure 20 inches square, and bind the cut edges with masking tape.

Yarn

You will need about 7 ounces of Persian wool; 3 ounces of it will be used for the background.

Additional Materials

square piece of felt, preferably about 48 inches wide

fringe to match felt, about 5½ yards

narrow velvet ribbon to match outer edge of needlepoint, about 2 yards long and ¼ inch wide

Enlarging and Transferring

Enlarge the design so that it measures 16 inches square. Center the enlarged design face up under the canvas and, using an indelible marker, trace it onto the canvas. Trace carefully in order to preserve the precise geometric form of each motif and its accompanying mirror image on the opposite side of the canvas.

Special Tips for Work

Stitch one complete quarter of the design first, following the graph in Figure 1. Use this quarter as a model for the rest of the design; the other three quarters repeat the same motifs in reverse, or "flopped," and should be worked to match (see Figure 2).

Around all four edges, extend the design two extra rows.

Finishing and Assembling

Block the needlepoint.

Sew a row of machine stitching on the excess canvas about ½ inch out from the needlepoint.

Cut the masking tape away on all four sides. There will be about 1½ inches of unstitched canvas all around (see Figure 3).

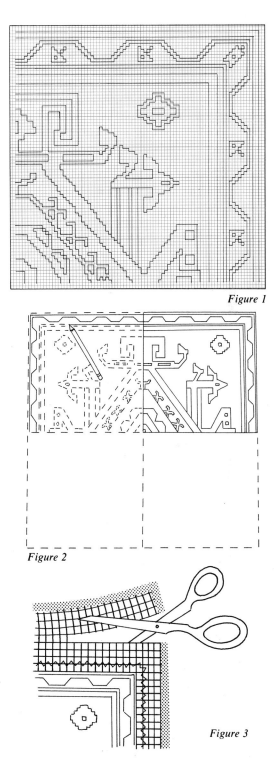

Figure 1

Figure 2

Figure 3

Note the exact measurements of the stitched design.

To prepare the felt square for the needlepoint insert, first find and mark the center point. Use that point as a focus, and, with a pencil, draw a square on the felt around it that is barely smaller than the stitched design (see Figure 4). Be sure that the square is evenly centered on the felt and that its sides

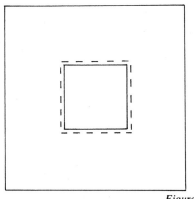

Figure 4

are perfectly straight. To remove the center square, cut from the center point out toward each corner and then cut along the sides of the square (see Figure 5).

Lay the needlepoint face up and place the

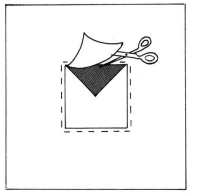

Figure 5

felt over it so that the square "window" frames the needlepoint (see Figure 6). It should cover the outer one or two rows of needlepoint. Make sure that the rows of stitching are straight, and then baste the edge

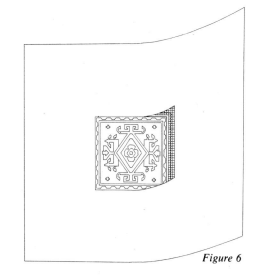

Figure 6

of the felt to the needlepoint; topstitch it with a machine. Finish with narrow velvet ribbon, blindstitching it on top of the join and neatly mitering it at the corners (see Figure 7).

Recheck to see that the needlepoint is cen-

Figure 7

tered on the felt; if not, trim the felt sides as necessary. Stitch the fringe around the bottom edges.

Decorating Bonus

If you want the card table cover to be fitted, shorten the side drop and sew box cor-

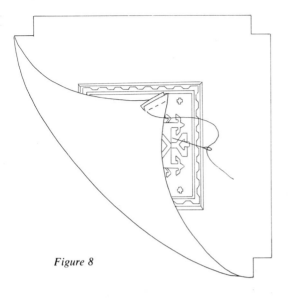

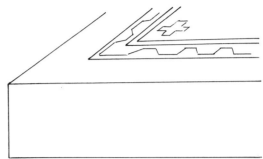

Figure 9

Figure 8

ners (see Figure 8). Or make a 2-foot-square hassock with a wide felt boxing strip (see Figure 9).

Leaf-Pattern Backgammon Board

The best game in town may well be played on this handsome backgammon board, its earthy colors and falling leaves inviting an autumnal match by the fire. This custom table (see "Sources") is the standard game-table height of 29 inches; the playing board is 22½ inches square. If you wish, lay the needlepoint game board in a Lucite or wooden gallery without a base and set it atop any of your own tables.

To make the needlepoint backgammon board, you will be using the following basic procedures, which have been described in detail in Section I:
- Preparing canvas
- Enlarging designs
- Transferring designs to canvas
- Stitching designs
- Blocking
- Mitering corners
- Lining

Stitch

Basketweave

Canvas

No. 10 mono
Cut one piece 26 inches square, and bind the edges with masking tape.

Yarn

You will need about 15½ ounces of Persian wool; 8½ ounces of it will be used for the background.

Additional Materials

thin fabric for lining

Enlarging and Transferring

Enlarge the design so that it measures 22½ inches square. Center the enlarged design face up under the canvas and, using an indelible marker, trace it onto the canvas.

Special Tips for Work

Around all four edges, extend the design one extra row.

Finishing and Assembling

Block the needlepoint.

Sew a row of machine stitching on the excess canvas about ½ inch out from the needlepoint.

Cut the excess canvas away on all four sides to within 1½ inches of the needlepoint, and cut the corners diagonally to within 1 inch of the stitching (see Figure 52).

Miter the four corners of the needlepoint and tack the excess canvas to the back of the stitching, making sure that the rows of needlepoint are perfectly straight and that no unstitched canvas shows along the edges (see Figure 56).

Lay the thin lining fabric over the mitered needlepoint, wrong sides together. Turn the lining under ½ inch on all four sides, and, mitering the corners when you come to them, blindstitch it to the back of the needlepoint (see Figure 67).

Adjusting the Design Area

Enlarge the square playing area to fit into any size square gallery.

Decorating Bonus

Make a dice cup, repeating the alternating green arrows (see Figure 1) by following the directions for the checked pencil holder (see page 173).

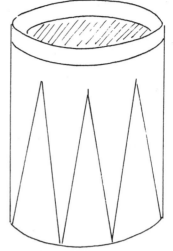

Figure 1

1 space = 1 inch

Chapter

4

Framed Pictures and Wall Hangings

Spring Floral Picture—directions on page 105.

Jungle Animal Scene—directions on page 107.

Needlepoint pictures are appealing in any size and location—a small colorful design can enliven a hall or powder room; a large picture can be the dramatic focus of a living room. The design can echo the colors or period of your decor or set it off in stunning contrast. Remember, too, that many art masterpieces, such as the Toulouse-Lautrec poster (see page 15), make splendid art objects themselves when translated into stitchery. In fact, transcribing a fine art design from one medium to another often provides a special understanding of both the design and the medium.

Any design can be framed for wall display. You might like to adapt a pattern from your home decor—perhaps from a fabric or china service—or to stitch a painting, poster, or drawing by a favorite artist. To adapt a design from any of these sources, see "Copying Designs" (page 15). Follow the directions below for mounting and framing your design.

Frames should enhance rather than compete with your needlepoint design. In general, simple frames are more effective than ornate ones. To avoid the cost of custom framing, try to find a ready-made frame before starting the project and then adjust measurements to frame.

Needlepoint pictures can be matted or not, depending on the frame and the desired effect. If used, mats should be cut with straight, rather than beveled edges. Mounting the work under glass is not necessary and may even hamper your enjoyment of the texture.

Spring Floral Picture

To make this framed picture, you will use the following basic procedures, which are described in detail in Section I:

- Preparing canvas
- Enlarging designs
- Transferring designs to canvas
- Stitching designs
- Blocking
- Protecting edges
- Mitering corners
- Lacing
- Lining

Stitch

Basketweave

Canvas

No. 12 mono
Cut one piece 18 inches square, and bind the edges with masking tape.

Yarn

You will need about 6 ounces of Persian wool; about 2½ ounces of it will be used for the background.

Additional Materials

Masonite for backing, 14 inches square
frame to fit Masonite
heavy brown paper for backing

Enlarging and Transferring

Enlarge the design so that it is 14 inches square. Center the enlarged design face up under the canvas and, using an indelible marker, trace it onto the canvas.

Special Tips for Work

Around all four sides, extend the design four extra rows.

Finishing and Assembling

Block the needlepoint.

Sew a row of machine stitching on the excess canvas about ½ inch out from the needlepoint.

Cut the excess canvas away on all four sides to within 1½ inches of the needlepoint, and cut the corners diagonally to within ½ inch of the stitching. Glue the cut edges and let dry (see Figure 1).

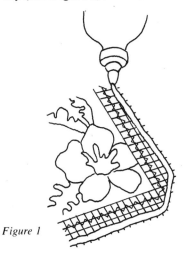

Figure 1

Lay the needlepoint face down and center the Masonite over it, making sure that the rows of stitching are straight. Temporarily anchor the needlepoint to the Masonite with tape (see Figure 57c).

Lace opposite sides of the canvas together with heavy carpet thread, starting in the center of the sides and working to within 2 inches of each corner (see Figure 60). Miter each corner and sew the mitered seams. Finish lacing opposite sides together.

Insert the mounted panel into the frame and secure it tightly with appropriate hardware or nails.

Cut heavy brown paper to mask the lacing and almost all of the frame and then glue it in place.

1 space = 1 inch

1 space = 1 inch

Jungle Animal Scene

To make this framed jungle animal picture, you will be using the following basic procedures, which have been described in detail in Section I:
- Preparing canvas
- Enlarging designs
- Transferring designs to canvas
- Stitching designs
- Blocking
- Protecting edges
- Mitering corners
- Lacing
- Lining

Stitch

Basketweave

Canvas

No. 12 mono
  Cut one piece of canvas to measure 24 inches square, and bind the cut edges with masking tape.

Yarn

  You will need about 6 ounces of Persian wool; about 3 ounces of it will be used for the background.

Additional Materials

Masonite, ¼ inch thick, 19 inches square, for backing
mat board, 19 inches square, natural color or color to complement needlepoint
frame to fit Masonite and mat board
heavy brown paper for backing

Enlarging and Transferring

  Enlarge the design so that it measures 14 inches square. Center the enlarged design face up under the canvas and, using an indelible marker, trace it onto the canvas.

Special Tips for Work

  Stitch the design without adding extra rows unless they are needed to fill the design out to a square.

Finishing and Assembling

  Block the needlepoint.
  Sew a row of machine stitching on the excess canvas about 1 inch in from the taped edges. Cut away the masking tape and cut the corners diagonally (see Figure 1). Glue the cut edges and let dry (see Figure 2).

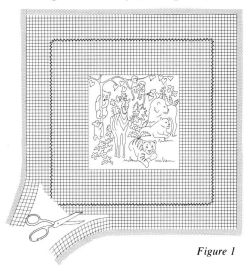

Figure 1

Figure 2

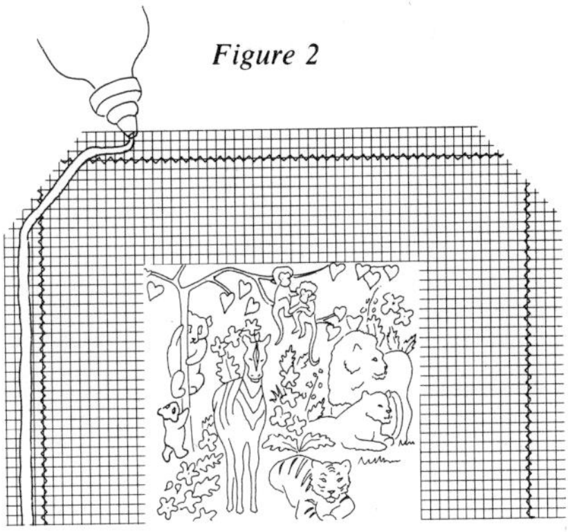

Lay the needlepoint face down and center the Masonite over it, making sure that the rows of stitching are straight. Temporarily anchor the needlepoint to the Masonite with tape (see Figure 3).

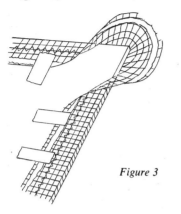

Figure 3

Lace opposite sides of the canvas together with heavy carpet thread, starting in the center of the sides and working to within 2 inches of each corner. Insert the needle into the canvas mesh behind the line of glue. Miter each corner and sew the mitered seams. Finish lacing opposite edges together (see Figure 4).

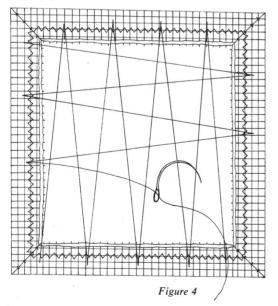

Figure 4

Cut a central window in the mat board to fit around the needlepoint exactly. It will be about 14 inches square and will lie over the unstitched canvas (see Figure 5). Secure it

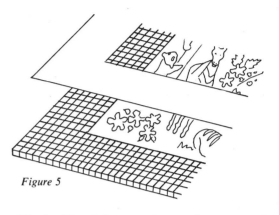

Figure 5

with double-stick tape. Insert the mounted panel into the frame and secure it with appropriate hardware or nails.

Cut heavy brown paper to cover the lacing and almost all of the frame. Glue it in place (see Figure 6).

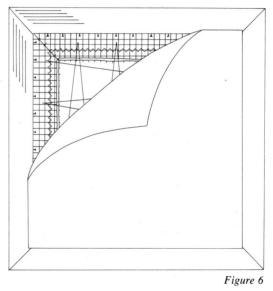

Figure 6

Art Nouveau Wall Hanging

An alternative to framing needlepoint pictures is to mount them unframed so that the freely hanging tapestry can display the soft textural qualities of the stitchery. This also has the claim of authenticity, since the earliest weavings were hung on walls and doors as protection against the weather.

This particular hanging derives from a French Art Nouveau poster by Paul Berthon. The hanging is virtually life-size and differs primarily from the poster in that the original flowers were lilies.

To make the Art Nouveau wall hanging, you will be using the following basic procedures, which have been described in detail in Section I:

- Preparing canvas
- Enlarging designs
- Transferring designs to canvas
- Stitching designs
- Blocking
- Protecting edges
- Mitering corners
- Lining

Stitch

Basketweave

Canvas

No. 12 mono
    Cut one piece 22 by 30 inches, and bind the edges with masking tape.

Yarn

You will need about 12 ounces of Persian wool.

Additional Materials

1 piece of velvet for backing, 25 by 34 inches
lining for velvet backing
3 strips of velvet for loops, each measuring 3 by 12 inches

lining for velvet loops
thin wooden slat, 22 inches long and ½ inch or less wide
dressmaker's weights

Enlarging and Transferring

Enlarge the design so that the width of the project will measure 18 inches; the length will measure about 26 inches. Center the enlarged design face up under the canvas and, using an indelible marker, trace it onto the canvas.

Special Tips for Work

Around all four edges, extend the design one extra row.

Finishing and Assembling

Block the needlepoint.
Sew a row of machine stitching on the

110

excess canvas about ½ inch out from the needlepoint.

Cut the excess canvas away on all four sides to within 1½ inches of the needlepoint, and cut the corners diagonally to within ½ inch of the stitching (see Figure 52).

Miter the four corners of the needlepoint and tack the excess canvas to the back of the stitching, making sure that the rows of stitching are perfectly straight and that no unstitched canvas shows along the edges (see Figure 56).

To make each of the three velvet loops, follow this procedure: Lay one of the velvet strips face down on its lining and sew the long side seams of both together, ½ inch in from the edges (see Figure 1). Turn the strip right side out and steam flat. Fold the fabric strip in half and stitch the open ends together ½ inch in from the ends (see Figure 2).

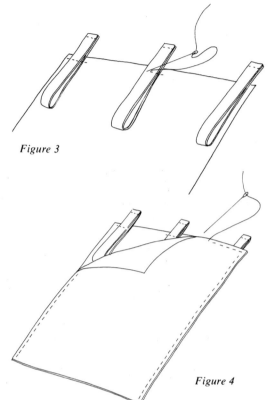

Figure 3

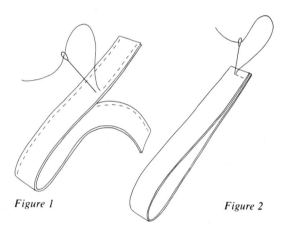

Figure 1   Figure 2

Figure 4

Lay the lining for the hanging face up. Place the loops on top of the lining with their raw ends extending 1½ inches beyond the edge of the lining. Place one loop at each end and one in the center (see Figure 3). Baste each of the loops securely in place.

Lay the large piece of velvet face down over the loops and lining. Baste and then sew the top and both sides together, leaving ½ inch seam allowance all around (see Figure 4).

Cut away the excess material at the cor-

ners and slip the wooden slat through the pockets in the loops (see Figure 5). Sew dressmaker's weights to the bottom of the lining about 1 inch from the edge.

Turn right side out and steam the seams flat. Turn the lining and the velvet under ½

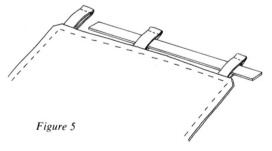

Figure 5

inch at the bottom and blindstitch together (see Figure 6).

Lay the needlepoint on velvet backing, centering from side to side but leaving a slightly wider border at bottom than top. Blindstitch to velvet.

Decorating Bonus

This project is an appropriate size for a fireplace screen (see page 134); the handsome design will provide an attractive focal point and conversation piece for your living room.

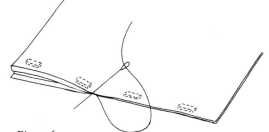

Figure 6

1 space = 1 inch

Birds-on-Ivy Bellpull

Most bellpulls no longer summon servants, but even after having lost their function, these long, narrow wall hangings are still in fashion.

To make this bellpull, you will use the following basic procedures, which are described in detail in Section I:

- Preparing canvas
- Enlarging designs
- Transferring designs to canvas
- Stitching designs
- Blocking
- Protecting edges
- Mitering corners
- Lining

Stitch

Basketweave

Canvas

No. 12 mono

Cut one piece 10 by 38 inches, and bind the edges with masking tape.

Yarn

You will need about 6 ounces of Persian wool; 4 ounces of it will be used for the background.

Additional Materials

felt for lining, the same width as the finished needlepoint and 3 inches longer
set of bellpull hardware with a minimum opening of 6½ inches

Enlarging and Transferring

Enlarge the design so that the width measures 6½ inches; the length will be about 34½ inches. Center the enlarged design face up under the canvas and, using an indelible marker, trace it onto the canvas.

Special Tips for Work

Around all four sides, extend the design one extra row.

Finishing and Assembling

Block the needlepoint.

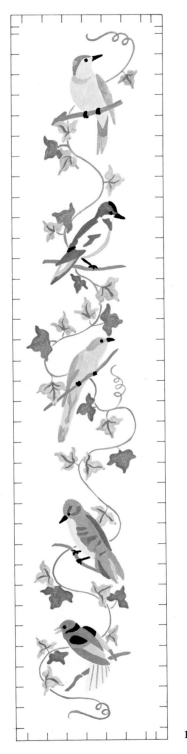

1 space = 1 inch

Sew a row of machine stitching on the excess canvas about ½ inch out from the needlepoint.

Cut the excess canvas away on all four sides to within 1½ inches of the neeldepoint, and cut the corners diagonally to within ½ inch of the stitching (see Figure 1).

Miter the four corners of the needlepoint and tack the excess canvas to the back of the stitching, making sure that the rows of stitching are straight and that no unstitched canvas shows along the edges (see Figure 56).

Center the needlepoint face up on the felt lining so that about 1½ inches of the lining extends at each end and blindstitch in place (see Figure 2). At each end, slip the felt tabs through the hardware and tack down securely (see Figure 3). Hang bellpull on a decorative hook.

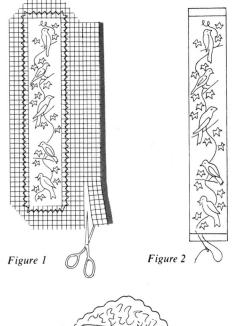

Figure 1   *Figure 2*

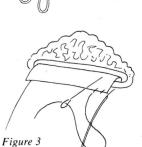

Figure 3

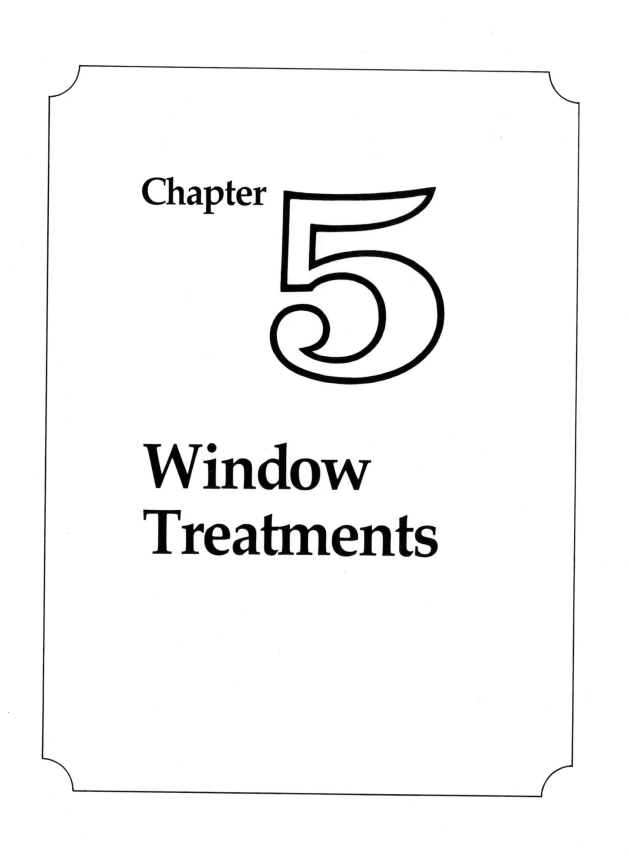

Chapter

5

Window Treatments

Bargello Valance

Valances lend graceful proportions to even the least imposing rooms. This handsome geometric design, derived from a nearby stair carpet and stitched in a combination of basketweave and gobelin, turned a small, square dining room into a charming area and tied it nicely into the nearby living space.

The needlepoint is mounted on a box valance board 46 inches wide, 10 inches high, and 6 inches deep. These proportions are appropriate for the window (41 by 55 inches) and for the length of the curtains (84 inches). Plan your own valance so that it is about 2 inches wider on each side than the window and so that its depth is from 1/9 to 1/6 the length of the curtains.

To make the needlepoint valance, you will use the following basic procedures, which are described in detail in Section I:

- Preparing canvas
- Transferring designs to canvas
- Stitching designs
- Blocking
- Protecting edges

Stitches

Basketweave for the triangles
Gobelin over one, two, and four threads for the linear design.

Remember to use the full three-strand thread when working any of the gobelin variations and two of the three strands for basketweave.

Canvas

No. 12 mono
Cut one piece so that it is 4 inches larger all around than the dimensions of the valance board, including the end boards. Bind the edges with masking tape.

Yarn

You will need about 3½ ounces of Persian

Design adapted from the carpet design "Media Metrics," courtesy Brintons Carpets (U.S.A.) Ltd.

wool for each square foot of design.

Additional Materials

box valance board of lightweight wood (the face should be made of plywood and the rest of ¾-inch pine)
thin cotton fabric for lining
cotton batting, cut to size of box face
angle irons to hang valance box

Enlarging and Transferring

Work the design from Figure 1, setting it up on your canvas so that the geometric figures fall evenly from top to bottom and from side to side. The pattern is easy to establish

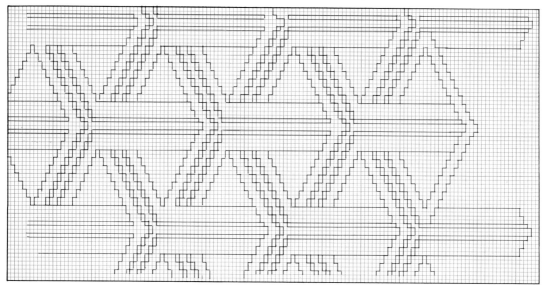

Figure 1

if you first stitch the straight lines or the diagonals across the whole canvas rather than completing each figure as you go. Fill the triangles in last with basketweave, tucking in an extra stitch where the basketweave meets the gobelin (see Figure 2).

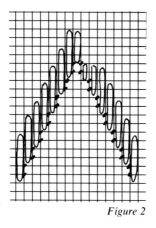

Figure 2

Special Tips for Work

Around all four edges, extend the design 1 inch. Then measure the needlepoint against the valance box to be sure that there is enough not only to cover but to turn under

and tack on the inside. You may find that additional stitching will be needed since the gobelin stitch sometimes "shrinks" the canvas slightly.

Finishing and Assembling

Block the needlepoint if necessary.

Sew a row of machine stitching on the excess canvas just outside the needlepoint.

Lay the cotton batting over the face board of the valance box. Cut one piece of lining 3 inches wider and longer than the valance board, including the two end sections as well as the face. Lay the lining over the padded face board and tack it as follows (see Figure 3): At the top, turn under a narrow hem in the lining and tack it to the board across the top and above the face (BF); repeat for both

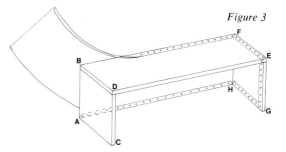

Figure 3

end sections (BD and FE). Take tucks or miter at the corners (B and F) as necessary. Smooth lining over the face board and, in the same manner, tack the lining to the inside across the bottom (AH) and then across each end section (AC and HG); cut excess material at inside corners H and A if necessary. Finally, hem and tack the end pieces (EG and DC).

Position the needlepoint on the padded valance box as follows (see Figure 4): Center

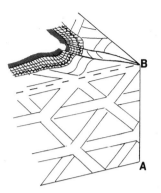

Figure 6

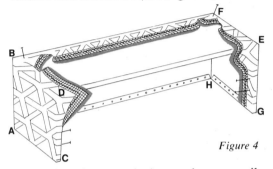

Figure 4

the needlepoint over the box and temporarily tack the ends to the inside of the end sections (EG and DC). Temporarily secure it at the top corners (B and F).

Permanently upholster the needlepoint as follows (see Figure 5): Tack the bottom of the needlepoint to the inside of the face board (HA). Pull it taut across the face board

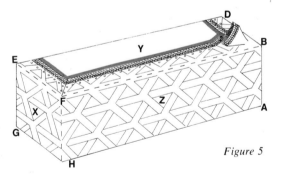

Figure 5

(Z) and tack it permanently to the top (Y) across the front edge (FB). Upholster each end section, again starting at the bottom and working to the top—tack GH, then EF, and, finally, EG. When you come to an outside corner, such as at B or F, miter the material (see Figure 6). When you come to an inside

corner, such as at A or H, don't be afraid to cut away any excess needlepoint in order to reduce bulk; glue cut edges (see Figure 7). Upholster the other end section in the same way. When the box has been upholstered, cut away the tape and unstitched canvas, leaving about 1 inch; glue the cut edges.

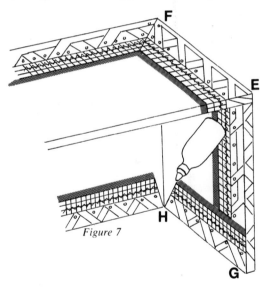

Figure 7

Finish lining the valance box as follows (see Figure 8): Lay the lining across the top (Y), turning under a narrow hem and tacking along BF, BD, and FE. Without cutting it, bring the lining across and then under the top, tacking it at the inside corners (F and B) and anchoring it across the bottom of the face board on the inside (AH). Along the bottom edge (AH), blindstitch it to the needlepoint with a curved needle. Cut two pieces of lining for the end sections (X); hem

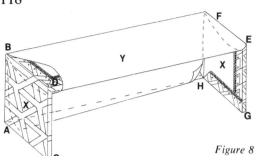

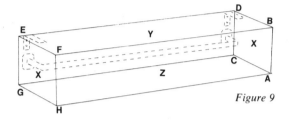

Figure 8

and tack them in the same manner to the inside edges.

Mount the valance board a few inches above the top of the window with angle irons; install your curtain hardware (see Figure 9).

Decorating Bonus

An upholstered valance makes a splendid heading for long or short hanging curtains. If you like drapes, consider the matching tiebacks that follow.

Figure 9

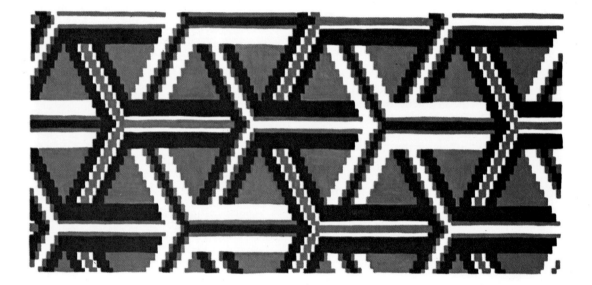

Bargello Drapery Tiebacks

The tiebacks on page 115 use one complete geometric form of the valance design enclosed in a black border to form a hexagonal medallion.

To make the tiebacks, you will use the following basic procedures, which are described in detail in Section I:

- Preparing canvas
- Transferring designs to canvas
- Stitching designs
- Blocking
- Protecting edges
- Hemming
- Lining

Stitches

Basketweave for the triangles
Gobelin over one, two, and four threads for the linear design.

Remember to use the full three-strand thread when working any of the gobelin variations and two of the three strands for basketweave.

Canvas

No. 12 mono

Cut two pieces of canvas, each 8 by 9 inches, and bind the edges with masking tape.

Yarn

You will need about ¾ ounce of Persian wool for one pair of tiebacks.

Additional Materials

2 pieces of felt for tiebacks (see Figure 1)
4 curtain rings and 2 hooks

Enlarging and Transferring

Work the design from Figure 2 on each piece of canvas.

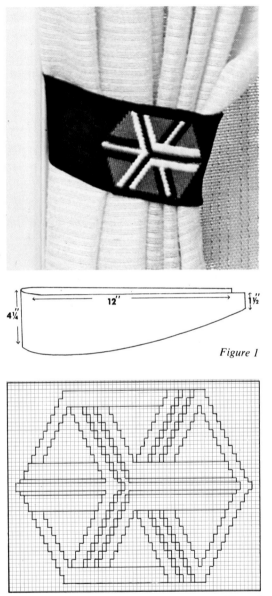

Figure 1

Figure 2

Finishing and Assembling

Block the needlepoint if necessary.
Around each hexagon, sew a row of ma-

chine stitching on the excess canvas just outside the needlepoint.

On all six sides, cut the excess canvas away to within ½ inch of the stitching. Hem the canvas to the back of the needlepoint, making tucks at the six points as needed (see Figure 3).

Fold one felt tieback in half and mount the needlepoint to the right of the fold. Blind-stitch in place. Sew rings to the ends of the tieback. Loop the tieback around the curtains and hang the rings on a hook mounted at the side of the window (see Figure 4). Mount the matching hexagon in reverse for the left tieback.

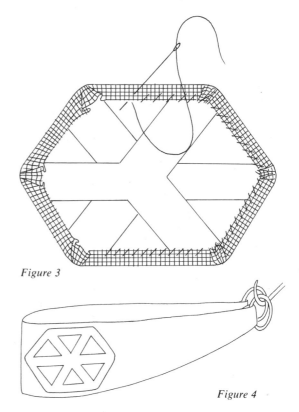

Figure 3

Decorating Bonus

If you want a less formal look, mount the needlepoint hexagons on 1-inch-wide ribbon or cord.

Figure 4

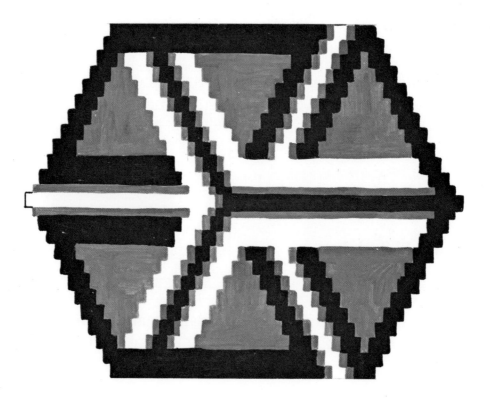

Pennsylvania Dutch Shade Trim

The easiest way to brighten a window is with shade trim. You can pick up a pattern or color already in the room or add a bright new touch as this hearts-and-flowers folk art design does.

To make the shade trim, you will use the following basic procedures, which are described in detail in Section I:

- Preparing canvas
- Enlarging designs
- Transferring designs to canvas
- Stitching designs
- Blocking

Stitches

Basketweave
Overcasting on edges

Canvas

No. 10 interlocking

Cut one piece so that it is 6 inches high and the width of your shade plus 4 inches. Bind the edges with masking tape.

Yarn

You will need about 1 ounce of Persian wool for each full repeat shown in the color guide.

Enlarging and Transferring

Enlarge the design so that the width measures 2½ inches; the length will be about 13⅓ inches.

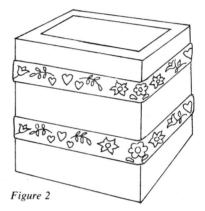

Figure 1

Place the enlarged design face up any-where under the canvas and, using an indel-ible marker, trace it onto the canvas. Then repeat the design as a whole or repeat any one of the daisy, heart, or tulip motifs on ei-ther side to the width of your window shade (see Figure 1), ''flopping'' the motifs for symmetry if you like.

Special Tips for Work

Around all four edges, work up to, but not including, the last row of the design.

Finishing and Assembling

Block the needlepoint.

Along all edges carefully cut the canvas one row outside the existing needlepoint, leaving one canvas thread remaining all around. Finish the edges with the over-casting stitch (see Figure 29).

With white glue, glue the finished strip along the bottom edge of your window shade and weight it with heavy books until dry.

Decorating Bonus

Dress up an ice bucket or planter with two strips of trim glued around the sides (see Figure 2).

Figure 2

1 space = 1 inch

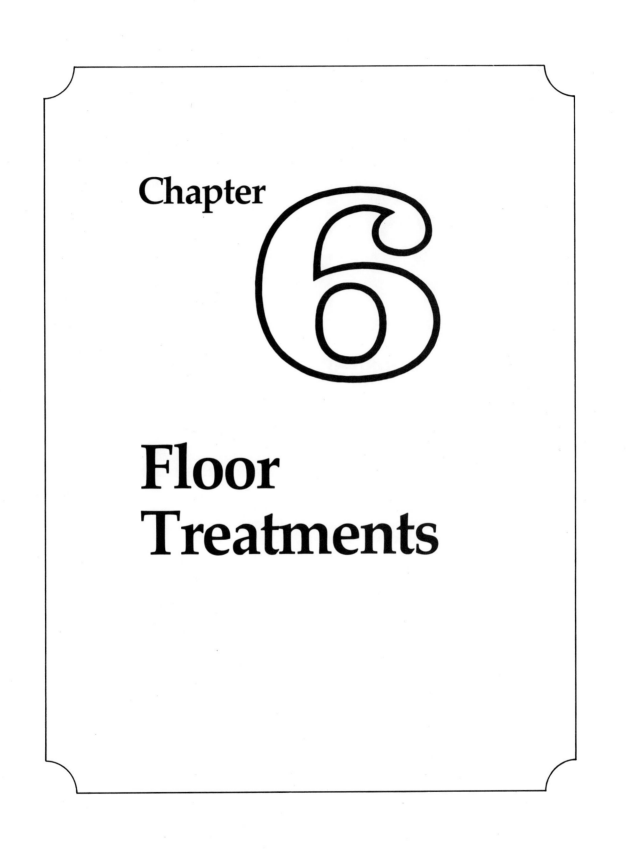

Chapter

6

Floor
Treatments

Chinese Dragon Rug

The motifs and colors of Oriental rugs are felicitous models for contemporary needlepoint, as shown by this harmonious design of Chinese origin. It is worked in five separate pieces—the two side strips with the border design; the top and bottom sections, each one incorporating part of the top and bottom borders; and the central dragon piece.

To make the Chinese Dragon rug, you will be using the following basic procedures, which have been described in detail in Section I:

- Preparing canvas
- Enlarging designs
- Transferring designs to canvas
- Stitching designs
- Joining
- Blocking
- Protecting edges
- Mitering corners
- Lining
- Cording

Stitch

Basketweave

Canvas

No. 10 mono

Making sure that the selvage runs vertically in every piece, cut five pieces of canvas as follows: two side strips, each 14 by 83 inches; top and bottom sections, each 35 by 32 inches; center section, 35 by 27 inches. Bind the edges with masking tape.

Yarn

You will need about 125 ounces of Persian

wool; about 75 ounces of it will be used for the background.

Additional Materials

lining for the joined rug, about 53 by 81 inches
thin nonskid rubber backing
thin cording, about 22 feet, to match the dark green outer border strip (optional)

Enlarging and Transferring

Enlarge the whole design so that the width measures 51 inches; the length will be about 79 inches.

Cut the enlarged design into its five working sections (see Figure 1). Center each design segment face up under its corresponding piece of canvas and, using an indelible marker, trace it onto its canvas. Each section will have about 2 inches of excess canvas around all four sides, which will be required for the subsequent joining of the five sections.

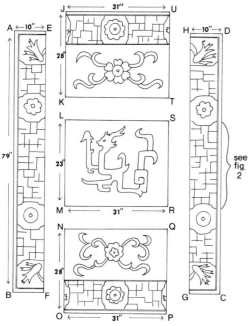

Figure 1

Special Tips for Work

Stitch the two long side strips first, extending the design two additional rows on all four sides of each strip. Work the fretwork as shown in Figure 2, which diagrams the longest section of fretwork (see the bracketed area in Figure 1). To work the shorter areas of fretwork in the borders, use as much of the diagram in Figure 2 as is needed to fill the area; work the same portion in reverse on the opposite border. When you have completed the side strips, note the number of rows lengthwise (from E to F and from H to G in Figure 1), including the two additional rows at each end.

Figure 2

Work the top and bottom sections, stitching two additional rows at the top and at the bottom (JU and OP in Figure 1) and at the sides (JK, UT, NO, and QP), but not at the interior edges (KT and NQ). Work the fretwork portions as shown in Figure 2, using as much of the design as is needed to fill the areas.

Work the center section last. On the two sides (LM and SR in Figure 1), add two extra rows for joining; on the top and bottom edges (LS and MR), leave seven rows of the design area unstitched. These will be stitched later in overlapping joins when the three center sections are assembled.

At this point the lengthwise line count should be rechecked to make sure that the total number of rows in the three center sections combined, including the fourteen rows to be stitched later, equals the number of rows in each side strip—that is, making sure that $EF=JK+LM+NO$. It is important to count the rows and not to rely on a tape measure. If any discrepancy has occurred, rectify it by increasing or decreasing the number of background rows in the center (dragon) section.

Finishing and Assembling

Block all five sections of the rug separately.

At the top and bottom of the center (dragon) section, cut off the excess canvas just outside the design (LS and MR in Figure 1), leaving the seven rows of unstitched mesh within the design area at the top and bottom.

On the inside edges of the top and bottom sections (KT and NQ in Figure 1), cut the excess canvas to within seven rows of the completed stitching; this will leave seven rows of unstitched mesh outside the design area.

Join the center section to the bottom section by using the overlapping method—that is, by laying the seven unstitched rows of the dragon section over the seven excess rows of the bottom section and joining them (see Figure 3). Complete the background area, stitching through the two thicknesses of canvas (see Figure 40). Join the center section to the top section by using the overlapping method as described above.

Around each side border and the newly joined center section, sew a row of machine

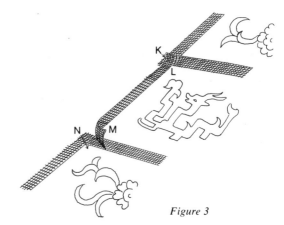

Figure 3

stitching on the excess canvas about ½ inch out from the needlepoint.

To the newly joined center section, seam one side border and then the other as follows: With right sides together, baste and then sew EF to JO and UP to HG. Stitch just inside the two extra rows of seam allowance, always matching rows. Trim the excess canvas outside the seam to about 1 inch and tack it down to the back of the stitching (see Figure 46).

Lay the joined rug face down. Cut the excess canvas away on all four sides to within 1½ inches of the needlepoint, and cut the corners diagonally to within 1 inch of the stitching (see Figure 4).

Miter the four corners of the needlepoint and tack the excess canvas to the back of the stitching, making sure that the rows of needlepoint are straight and that no unstitched canvas shows along the edges (see Figure 56).

Lay the lining over the hemmed rug and anchor it in a few places with basting stitches. On three sides, turn the lining under so that it just meets the needlepoint and blindstitch it to the back of the needlepoint. Miter the corners as you come to them (see Figure 67). On the fourth side, hem the lining without sewing it to the needlepoint; it will hang loose like the hem of a lined dress, enabling you to shake or vacuum away any dirt or dust. Remove basting.

To all four corners of the lining, sew strips

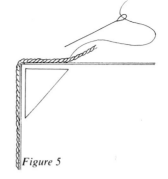

Figure 5

Figure 4

or triangles of nonskid rubber backing.

If you want a more finished edge and extra protection against wear, blindstitch cording around the four edges of the rug (see Figure 5).

Adjusting the Design Area

To alter the size of the rug, you can stitch more or less background area or you can use any one of the field motifs, eliminating the other two entirely. The only essential is to plan the borders first—especially the fretwork—by count and then to fit the design of the field into that area.

Decorating Bonus

Many of the rug motifs can be picked up and used in other projects for interesting results—the border medallions in round pillows, one or more field motifs in a wall hanging, the fretwork border as shade trim, and the shades of green plus the red as accent in a bargello footstool.

1 space = 1 inch

Forest-Scene Inlaid Rug

Nothing lifts an expanse of commercial carpeting out of the ordinary like an inset of needlepoint. Whatever the shape of the stitched area—round, square, triangular, irregular, or rectangular, as in this hearth rug —it quickly customizes a ready-made rug. Its obvious decorating value is to make a large impact with minimal stitching. It offers intriguing possibilities for floor treatments for an entrance hall, for example, where a mat could carry needlepoint insets spaced out of the way of heavy traffic; it could also be done as a bedroom area rug with the inlaid needlepoint section providing a border around the bed.

This particular rug is designed for a hearth, where its autumnal colors and natural woodsy forms provide an appropriate fireside setting. The central needlepoint area is stitched and then set into a ready-made pile rug.

To make this rug, you will use the following basic procedures, which are described in detail in Section I:
- Preparing canvas
- Enlarging designs
- Transferring designs to canvas
- Stitching designs
- Blocking
- Mitering corners

Stitch

Basketweave

Canvas

No. 10 penelope

Cut one piece 34 by 22 inches, and bind the edges with masking tape.

Yarn

You will need about 17 ounces of Persian wool; about 7 ounces of it will be used for the background.

Additional Materials

pile rug or carpet, measuring 42 by 30 inches to provide a 6-inch frame around the needlepoint.

Enlarging and Transferring

Enlarge the design so that the width measures 30 inches; the height will be about 18 inches.

Center the enlarged design face up under the canvas and, using an indelible marker, trace it onto the canvas.

Special Tips for Work

For finer detail, you can stitch the snake, butterflies, ladybugs, and acorn shells in petit point by splitting the two thread canvas; see "Tips for Stitching" (page 24).

Around all four edges, extend the design for one extra row.

Finishing and Assembling

Block the needlepoint.

Sew a row of machine stitching on the excess canvas about ½ inch out from the needlepoint.

Cut the excess canvas away on all four sides to within 1½ inches of the nedlepoint, and cut the corners diagonally to within 1 inch of the stitching (see Figure 52).

Miter the four corners of the needlepoint and tack the excess canvas to the back of the stitching, making sure that the rows of stitching are straight and that no unstitched canvas shows along the edges (see Figure 56). Take exact measurements of the finished piece).

To prepare the rug for the needlepoint inset, shave the pile from a rectangular area in the center of the rug that is the same size as the finished needlepoint. To do this, use a single-edged razor blade and shave the pile as close as you can, working until you see the backing of the rug between the stumps of the original rug knots; these cannot be removed and should be ignored.

Apply double-stick carpet tape to the back of the needlepoint, making sure to cover the corners and edges well. Press the needlepoint into the prepared rug (see Figure 1).

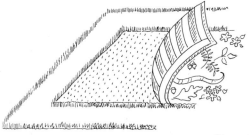

Figure 1

Adjusting the Design Area

The easiest way to alter the size of the project is to use a smaller or larger pile rug. If you want the needlepoint itself to be smaller, work the needlepoint design on No. 12 or No. 14 mono canvas, which will reduce its overall dimensions.

Decorating Bonus

Shape the pile rug to frame your fireplace and repeat sections of the design in the side pieces (see Figure 2).

Figure 2

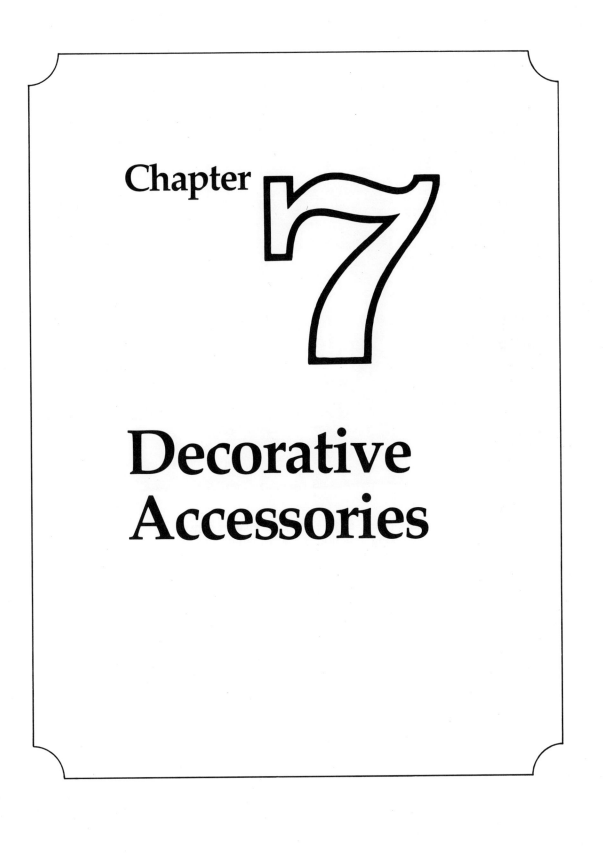

Chapter **7**

Decorative Accessories

Japanese Fireplace Screen

Fireplaces are prized in any room, and because their heating and cooking functions have long since been moved to other locations in the home, their empty hearths invite special decorative attention. A needlepoint fire screen is an admirable solution. Its prominent location makes a splendid showcase for an unusual design, and it will deflect any stray gusts of wind that penetrate the flue.

This particular fireplace screen carries out the Oriental lines of the antique frame in a serene Japanese scene. The central needlepoint panel is mounted on a board and then inserted into the screen like a picture frame.

To make the fireplace screen, you will use the following basic procedures, which are described in detail in Section I:

- Preparing canvas
- Enlarging designs
- Transferring designs to canvas
- Stitching designs
- Blocking
- Protecting edges
- Mitering corners
- Lacing
- Lining

Stitch

Basketweave

Canvas

No. 12 mono

Cut one piece of canvas 15 by 19 inches, and bind the edges with masking tape.

Yarn

You will need about 4½ ounces of Persian wool.

Additional Materials

Masonite, ¼-inch, 11 by 15 inches
felt or heavy paper for backing

Enlarging and Transferring

Enlarge the design so that the width measures 11 inches; the height will be about 15 inches.
Center the design face up under the taped canvas and, using an indelible marker, trace it onto the canvas.

Special Tips for Work

Around all four sides, extend the design two extra rows.

Finishing and Assembling

Block the needlepoint.
Sew a row of machine stitching on the excess canvas just outside the needlepoint.
Cut the excess canvas away on all four sides to within 1½ inches of the needlepoint, and cut the corners diagonally to within ½ inch of the stitching (see Figure 52). Glue the cut edges and let dry.
Lay the needlepoint face down and center the Masonite over it. Temporarily anchor the needlepoint to the board with fabric tape (see Figure 1), making sure that the rows of stitching are straight.
Lace opposite sides of the canvas together with heavy carpet thread, starting in the center of the sides and working to within 2 inches of each corner (see Figure 60). Miter each corner and sew the mitered seams. Finish lacing the opposite edges together.
Insert mounted panel into fireplace screen and secure with appropriate hardware or

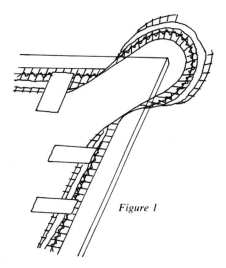

Figure 1

nails. Cut a piece of felt or heavy paper to fit back of frame; glue in place.

Adjusting the Design Area

To adjust the fit for your own fireplace screen, you can simply eliminate any part of the design that falls outside the dotted lines in Figure 2. Remember that since two or three rows of the design will be hidden by the lip of the frame, you will need to add these in addition to the two rows needed for mounting and lacing.

Figure 2

Decorating Bonus

If you can't find an interesting fireplace screen, make your own by mounting a large picture frame on a stand, using a single-pedestal type or double legs (see Figure 3).

Figure 3

1 space = 1 inch

Abstract Luggage-Rack Straps

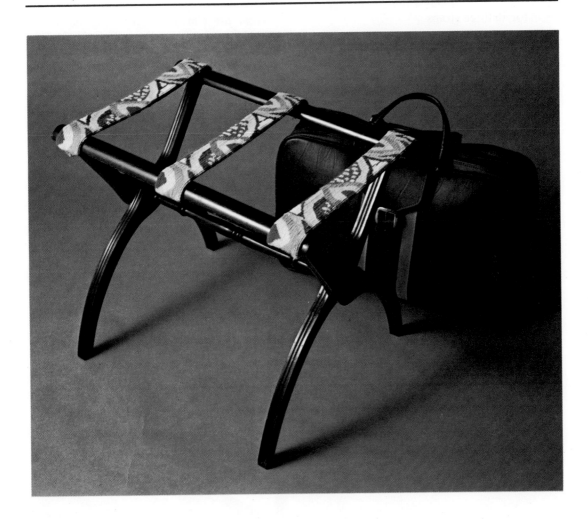

Welcome guests with a Pucci-like print to enliven your guest room. The straps need not be the same width or length as those now on your luggage rack; these will replace the old straps.

To make the straps, use the following procedures, described in Section I:
- Preparing canvas
- Enlarging designs
- Transferring designs to canvas
- Stitching designs
- Blocking
- Protecting edges
- Lining

Stitch

Basketweave

Canvas

No. 10 mono
   Cut three pieces, each 5 by 29 inches, and bind the edges with masking tape.

Yarn

You will need about 4 ounces of Persian wool for all three straps.

Additional Materials

ribbon for lining, 2 inches wide and 7 feet long

Enlarging and Transferring

Enlarge the design so that the width measures 2¼ inches; the length will be about 19 inches.

Center the enlarged design face up under each strip of canvas and, using an indelible marker, trace it onto the canvas.

Special Tips for Work

Along the long edges of all three strips, extend the design one extra row.

Finishing and Assembling

Block the needlepoint.

On each strap, sew a row of machine stitching on the excess canvas just outside the needlepoint.

Cut away the excess canvas on the long sides to within 1 inch of the needlepoint; on the short sides, cut just the tape away (see Figure 1).

Hem the canvas on the long sides with carpet thread, sewing through the back of the needlepoint as well as the unstitched canvas at the ends (see Figure 2).

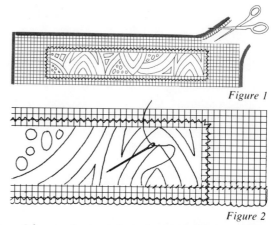

Figure 1

Figure 2

Line each strap entirely with ribbon, blind-stitching it to the back of the needlepoint and basting it to the unstitched canvas at the ends (see Figure 3).

Turn your luggage rack upside down and remove the existing straps. Tack or nail one end of a new strap to the bottom of one of the bars near, but not into, the old nail holes.

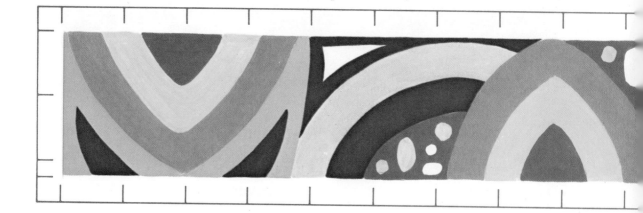

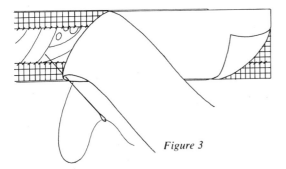

Figure 3

Wrap the strap (this will be mostly the un-stitched canvas end) entirely around the bar once and then bring it up and over the bar to the other side (see Figure 4). Wrap around the opposite bar in the same manner and nail

to correspond (see Figure 5). Repeat for the other two straps, spacing them evenly along the luggage rack bars.

Decorating Bonus

Transform a fourth strap length into a tie holder by doubling the needlepoint and then nailing it with a decorative tack to the guest closet door (see Figure 6).

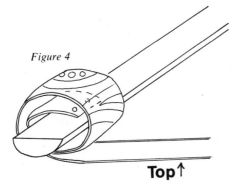

Figure 4

Top↑

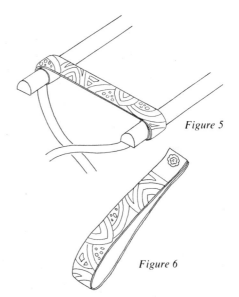

Figure 5

Figure 6

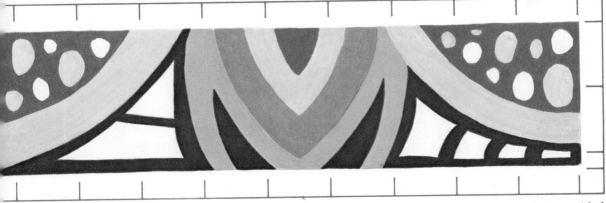

1 space = 1 inch

Flowered Picture Frame

Frame your favorite photograph with needlepoint and display both in a clear acrylic "sandwich" (see "Sources"). This particular design, which derives from the contemporary fabric shown in the pillow, can be adapted to fit practically any decorating scheme.

To make the needlepoint panel, you will use the following basic procedures, which are described in detail in Section I:

- Preparing canvas
- Enlarging designs
- Transferring designs to canvas
- Stitching designs
- Blocking
- Protecting edges
- Mitering corners
- Lining

Stitch

Basketweave

Canvas

No. 12 mono

Cut one piece 14 by 16 inches, and bind the edges with masking tape.

Yarn

You will need about 2 ounces of Persian wool; about 1⅓ ounces of it will be used for the background.

Additional Materials

clear frame, 10 by 12 inches, made up of two pieces of ¼-inch-thick acrylic, each with ⅜-inch holes drilled ½ inch in from each of the four corners; and a triangular stand glued to the back of one of the pieces (see Figure 1)

4 headless threaded screws, ¼ inch in diameter and 1½ inches long

4 nuts

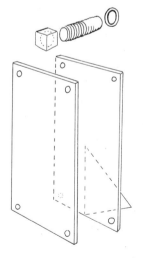

Figure 1

4 decorative square chrome heads with threads
stiff cardboard, 8½ by 10½ inches
felt for lining

Enlarging and Transferring

Enlarge the design so that the width measures 9½ inches; the height will be about 11½ inches.

Center the enlarged design face up under the prepared canvas and, using an indelible marker, trace it onto the canvas.

Special Tips for Work

Stitch to the edge of the design without adding any extra rows. Leave the center rectangle unstitched—it will measure about 4¼ by 6¼ inches—and do not cut it. Your photograph will be mounted right on top of the unstitched canvas mesh.

Finishing and Assembling

Block the needlepoint.

Sew a row of machine stitching on the excess canvas about ½ inch out from the needlepoint.

Cut the excess canvas away on all four sides to within 1½ inches of the needlepoint, and cut the corners diagonally to within 1 inch of the stitching.

Lay the needlepoint face down and center the cardboard over it. Temporarily anchor the needlepoint to the edge of the cardboard with stick pins, making sure that the rows of stitching are straight (see Figure 2).

With all-purpose white resin glue, stick opposite sides of the canvas to the cardboard, starting in the center of the sides and working to within 2 inches of each corner. Cover the glued area with wax paper and weight it with a heavy book until the glue has dried.

Miter each corner and glue all edges onto the cardboard. Weight down as above and let dry (see Figure 3). Cut felt lining to size and

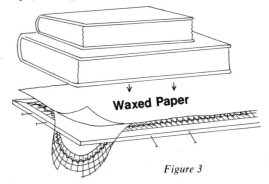

Waxed Paper

Figure 3

glue to back. Weight down and let dry.

Mount your favorite 5-by 7-inch photograph on the center unstitched canvas mesh with double-stick tape, cutting off the white picture border if necessary.

To assemble the frame thread the long screws into the decorative chrome heads, insert the mounted photograph between the

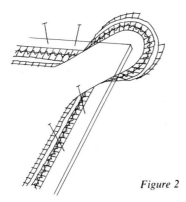

Figure 2

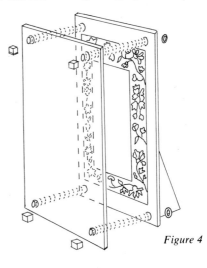

Figure 4

two sheets of acrylic, push the screws through the holes from the front, and secure them at the rear with the four nuts (see Figure 4). If the screws protrude, saw them off so that they are flush with the back of the nuts.

Decorating Bonus

Since the clear plastic actually extends beyond the needlepoint on all four sides, you can provide a colored "mat" by using an opaque or translucent back sheet.

1 space = 1 inch

Landscape Planter Jacket

Turn a planter cube into an elegant cachepot by encasing it in a snug-fitting needlepoint sleeve. This abstract design clothes a planted 5-inch plastic cube.

To make the planter jacket, you will use the following basic procedures, which are described in detail in Section I:

- Preparing Canvas
- Enlarging designs
- Transferring designs to canvas
- Stitching designs
- Blocking
- Protecting edges
- Joining
- Hemming

Stitch

Basketweave

Canvas

No. 12 mono
Cut one pice 24 by 11 inches, and bind the edges with masking tape.

Yarn

You will need about 3½ ounces of Persian wool.

Enlarging and Transferring

Enlarge the design so that the width measures 20 inches; the height will be about 6½ inches.

Center the enlarged design face up under the canvas and, using an indelible marker, trace it onto the canvas.

Special Tips for Work

Along the top and bottom (the long edges), extend the design one extra row. On the sides (the short edges), stop the design one thread short of the outline (see Figure 1).

Figure 1

Finishing and Assembling

Block the needlepoint.

Sew a row of machine stitching on the excess canvas just outside the design outline.

Cut the excess canvas away on all four sides to within 1 inch of the needlepoint (see Figure 2).

Check the width of the needlepoint against the perimeter of the cube. If they are the same size, finish the cube with a butt join. If the needlepoint is wider than the perimeter, use the seam join described below.

For the butt join, turn the excess canvas to the back on each short edge, leaving just one row of canvas thread showing on each end (see Figure 43). Bring the ends together and baste the two threads together, matching rows. Using appropriate color yarn, work over the basted row with a vertical outline stitch to complete the design (see Figure 45). Hem the excess canvas at the back of the join to the inside of the needlepoint (see Figure 46).

For a seam join, place the two ends right sides together and baste along a fitted seam line, carefully matching the rows (see Figure 33). Sew over the basting by machine. Hem the excess canvas to the back of the join and turn right side out.

Along the top and bottom edges, turn the excess canvas to the inside and hem it to the

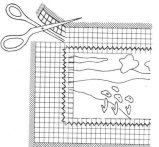

Figure 2

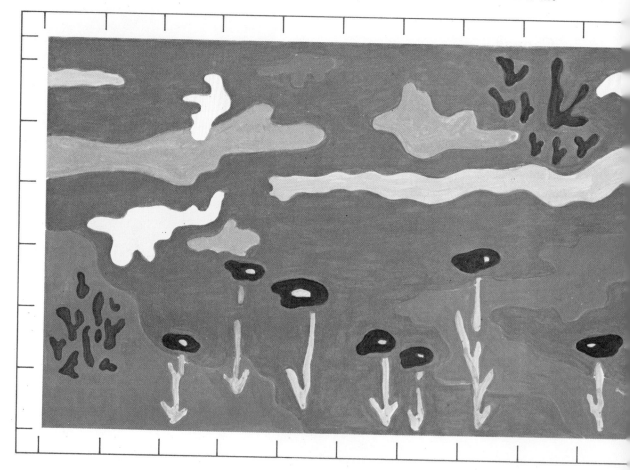

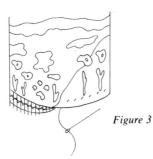

Figure 3

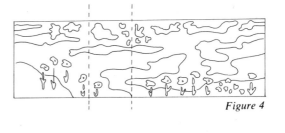

Figure 4

Figure 5

back of the needlepoint (see Figure 3). Pull the needlepoint sleeve over the cube, positioning the seam over one corner.

Adjusting the Design Area

To make a shorter or narrower plant holder cover, omit as much of the design as necessary between the dotted lines in Figure 4. To make a larger cover, extend the design as shown in Figure 5.

Decorating Bonus

If you don't have a green thumb but you love the design, make it for the ice bucket on page 159.

1 space = 1 inch

Rose-Pattern Lamp Base

A dainty rosebud print encases this pretty Lucite lamp base, a charming item for a boudoir or young girl's room. This particular lamp base (see "Sources") is double-walled to enclose the needlepoint, but the same needlepoint "sleeve" could upholster a wooden column wired as a lamp.

To make the needlepoint panel, you will use the following basic procedures, which are described in detail in Section I:
- Preparing canvas
- Enlarging designs
- Transferring designs to canvas
- Stitching designs
- Blocking
- Protecting edges
- Joining
- Hemming

Stitch

Basketweave

Canvas

No. 10 penelope
Cut one piece 13 by 12 inches, and bind the edges with masking tape.

Yarn

You will need over 2 ounces of Persian wool.

Enlarging and Transferring

Enlarge the design so that the width measures 8¾ inches; the height will be about 7¾ inches.

Center the enlarged design face up under the canvas and, using an indelible marker, trace it onto the canvas.

Special Tips for Work

Work the design details—roses, stems,

leaves—in small stitches by dividing the penelope canvas into smaller mesh (see Figure 3 on page 11). Work the background in 10-to-the-inch stitches except in places where the design details intervene; around those details, complete the background in the small stitches until you can resume the larger stitches.

Along the top and bottom (long edges), extend design one extra row. On the sides (short edges), extend it two extra rows.

Finishing and Assembling

Block the needlepoint.

Sew a row of machine stitching on the excess canvas just outside the needlepoint.

Cut the excess canvas away on all four sides to within 1 inch of the needlepoint.

Place the two ends (the shorter edges) with right sides together and baste along the seam line, carefully matching the rows (see Figure 1). Baste and then sew the seam. Hem the excess canvas to the back of the needlepoint and turn right side out.

Figure 1

Turn the excess canvas at the top and bottom edges to the inside, and hem to the back of the needlepoint (see Figure 2). Slip the needlepoint into the lamp.

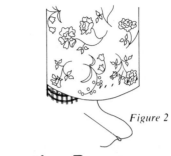

Figure 2

Decorating Bonus

Avoid the expense of a plastic lamp base by covering a 12-ounce soft drink can that has been wired for a lamp. Enlarge the design so that the width measures 8¾ inches; the height will be about 7¾ inches, but you should stitch just 4¾ inches of it (see Figure 3). Make the cover as described above.

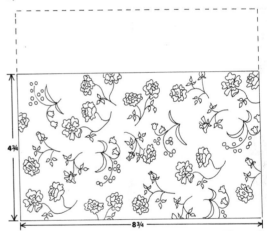

Figure 3

148

1 space = 1 inch

Scrollwork Mirror Frame

The charm of a needlepoint mirror frame rests in part on the contrast between the reflective sparkle of glass and the soft texture of wool.

To make this mirror frame, you will use the following basic procedures, which are described in detail in Section I:

- Preparing canvas
- Enlarging designs
- Transferring designs to canvas
- Stitching designs
- Blocking
- Protecting edges
- Mitering corners
- Lacing
- Lining

Stitch

Basketweave

Canvas

No. 12 mono
Cut one piece 17 by 21 inches, and bind the edges with masking tape.

Yarn

You will need about 4 ounces of Persian wool; 3 ounces of it will be used for the background.

Additional Materials

plywood, ¼ inch thick, the size of finished needlepoint (about 13 by 16¾ inches)
felt or heavy paper for lining
lightweight mirror, cut to size after blocking (it will be about 7¼ by 11 inches)

Enlarging and Transferring

Enlarge the design so that the width measures 12¼ inches; the height will be about 16 inches. Center the enlarged design face up under the taped canvas and, using an indelible marker, trace it onto the canvas.

Special Tips for Work

Leave the center rectangle unstitched—it will measure about 7¼ by 10¾ inches—and do not cut it. The mirror will be mounted on top of the canvas mesh.

Around all four edges, extend the design four extra rows.

Finishing and Assembling

Block the needlepoint.

Sew a row of machine stitching on the excess canvas just outside the needlepoint.

Cut the excess canvas away on all four sides to within 1½ inches of the needlepoint, and cut the corners diagonally to within 1 inch of the stitching. Glue the cut edges and let dry (see Figure 1).

Figure 1

Figure 2

Lay the needlepoint face down and center the plywood board over it. Temporarily anchor the needlepoint to the edge of the plywood with thin tacks (see Figure 57a), making sure that the rows of stitching are straight.

Lace opposite sides of the canvas together with heavy carpet thread, starting in the center of the sides and working to within 2 inches of each corner (see Figure 60). Miter each corner and sew the mitered seams. Finish lacing the opposite edges together.

When the needlepoint frame has been mounted, take it to a glazier for a lightweight mirror cut exactly to fit. It need not have polished edges.

Glue the mirror to the unstitched canvas mesh (see Figure 2), using an adhesive such as Black Magic Tough Glue, that will protect the silver backing on the mirror.

Cut felt or heavy paper to fit the back of the panel and glue in place. Attach appropriate hardware for hanging.

Decorating Bonus

Make a second "frame," but substitute a bargello design for the mirror (see Figure 3) and use shades from the blue and green family in the border.

Figure 3

1 space = 1 inch

Garden Tray Hanger

If you like to utilize odd pockets of space for storage, you will be delighted with this pair of straps for storing trays and place mats. Hang it on the refrigerator with a magnetic hook or out of the way behind the kitchen door. The design of the hanger echoes the colors and shapes of kitchen wallpaper; substitute your own kitchen colors.

To make the tray hanger, you will use the following basic procedures, which are described in detail in Section I:
- Preparing canvas
- Enlarging designs
- Transferring designs to canvas
- Stitching designs
- Blocking
- Lining

Stitch

Basketweave
Overcasting on edges

Canvas

No. 12 interlocking
Cut two pieces, each 6 by 23 inches, and bind the edges with masking tape.

Yarn

You will need about 1¼ ounces of Persian wool for each of the two mirror-image luggage straps.

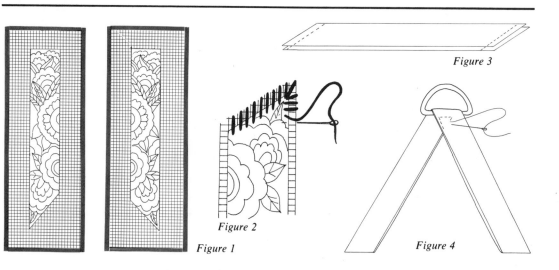

Figure 3

Figure 2

Figure 1

Figure 4

Additional Materials

2 lengths of grosgrain ribbon, each 46 inches
    long and 2¼ inches wide
"Dee" ring, 2½ inches in diameter

Enlarging and Transferring

Enlarge the design so that the width measures 2½ inches; the length will be about 19 inches at the point. Center the enlarged design face up under one strip of canvas and, using an indelible marker, trace it onto the canvas. Then trace the design in reverse on the other strip (see Figure 1).

Special Tips for Work

Around all edges, work up to, but not including, the last row of the design.

Finishing and Assembling

Block the needlepoint.

Along all edges, carefully cut the canvas one row outside the existing needlepoint, leaving one thread all around. Finish the edges with the overcasting stitch, working across the diagonal ends in the same manner as the sides (See Figure 2).

Prepare the ribbons as follows: Cut the

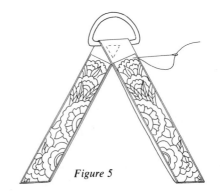

Figure 5

ends diagonally to match the points of the needlepoint and then seam the two ribbons together (see Figure 3). Turn right side out and pull the joined strips of ribbon through the dee ring until both tails are even. Spread the tails apart until their diagonally cut ends are parallel to the floor and then temporarily pin them together in that position. Sew a triangle through all layers just below the dee ring to secure in place permanently (see Figure 4).

Blindstitch the needlepoint panels to the top ribbon of each tail (see Figure 5).

Decorating Bonus

Trim your kitchen window shade with duplicate needlepoint strips (see page 121).

1 space = 1 inch

Butterfly Serving Tray

Wing drinks to your guests on a flutter of butterflies beguilingly caught in a clear plastic tray. In this particular tray (see "Sources"), the needlepoint nestles between the tray itself and a close-fitting protective plastic panel. You could improvise virtually the same effect by framing the needlepoint under glass and attaching a pair of handles at the ends.

To make the needlepoint tray insert, you will use the following basic procedures, which are described in detail in Section I:

- Preparing canvas
- Enlarging designs
- Transferring designs to canvas
- Stitching designs
- Blocking
- Protecting edges
- Mitering corners
- Lining

Stitch

Basketweave

Canvas

No. 12 mono
Cut one piece 17 by 23 inches, and bind the edges with masking tape.

Yarn

You will need about 6½ ounces of Persian

wool; 3½ ounces of it will be used for the background.

Additional Materials

thin fabric for lining

Enlarging and Transferring

Enlarge the design so that the width measures 13 inches; the length will be about 19 inches.

Center the enlarged design face up under the canvas and, using an indelible marker, trace it onto the canvas.

Special Tips for Work

Around all four sides, extend the design one extra row.

Finishing and Assembling

Block the needlepoint.

Sew a row of machine stitching on the excess canvas about ½ inch out from the needlepoint.

Cut the excess canvas away on all four sides to within 1½ inches of the needlepoint, and cut the corners diagonally to within 1 inch of the stitching.

Miter the four corners of the needlepoint and tack the excess canvas to the back of the stitching, making sure that the rows of stitching are straight and that no unstitched canvas shows along the edges.

Lay the lining over the mitered needlepoint, wrong sides together. Turn the lining under ½ inch on all four sides, mitering the corners as you work, and blindstitch to the back of the needlepoint (see Figure 67).

Adjusting the Design Area

If your own tray is larger and of different shape, outline its dimensions, enlarge the design, and then fill in any empty areas by repeating one or more of the butterflies traced from the enlarged design (see Figure 1). If your own tray is smaller, outline in proper proportion any section of the design that pleases you and enlarge it to size (see Figure 2).

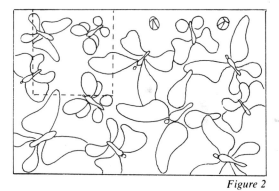

Figure 1

Figure 2

Decorating Bonus

Stitch single butterflies for coasters; make them 4 inches square on interlocking canvas and finish the edges with the overcasting stitch.

1 space = 1 inch

Monogrammed Napkin Rings

One ecologically sound gesture is to replace your paper dinner napkins with linen ones; then tuck them into needlepoint napkin rings that you have initialed to designate family members. These particular rings use the alphabet on pages 184 and 185 set into four different stripe patterns.

To make the napkin rings, you will use the following basic procedures, which are described in detail in Section I:
- Preparing canvas
- Transferring designs to canvas
- Stitching designs
- Joining
- Blocking
- Protecting edges
- Hemming

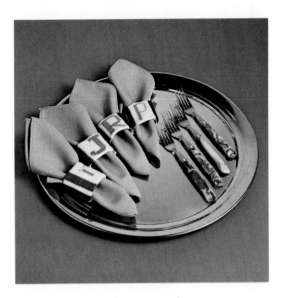

Stitch

Basketweave

Canvas

No. 12 mono

Cut one piece 9 by 4 inches for each napkin ring, and bind the edges with masking tape.

Yarn

You will need almost ½ ounce of Persian wool for each napkin ring

Additional Materials

ribbon, 6½ inches long and 2 inches wide for each napkin ring

Enlarging and Transferring

Each napkin ring is twenty-five rows wide and seventy-one or seventy-two stitches long (depending on the letter of the alphabet). If your initial has an even number of stitches to its width, make the central white block twenty-two stitches wide; if it has an uneven number to its width, make the central white block twenty-one stitches wide. Center the initial—whether capital or lowercase—in the white block and center the block on the canvas.

Special Tips for Work

Using any or all of the stripe patterns in Figure 1, work the entire design except for the end stripe enclosed by the bracket in each pattern.

Along the top and bottom edges, extend the design one extra row.

Finishing and Assembling

When you have completed all the stitching except for the bracketed end stripe, block the needlepoint.

Along the top and bottom edges, sew a row of machine stitching about ¼ inch outside the needlepoint.

Cut the masking tape away on the top and bottom, leaving 1 inch of excess canvas.

158

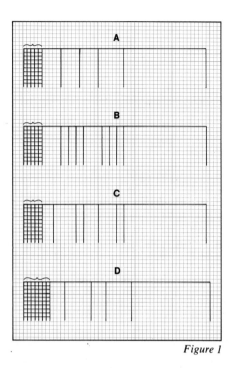

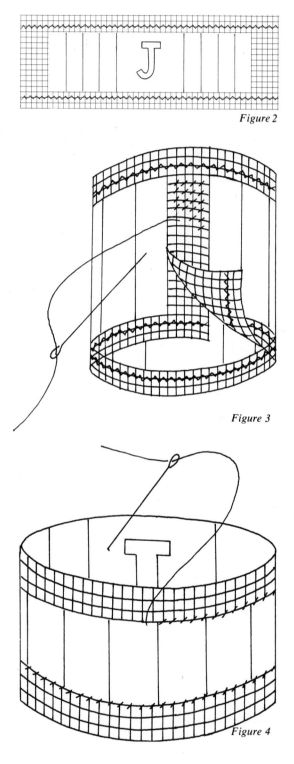

Figure 1

Figure 2

Figure 3

Figure 4

On each short end, cut the excess canvas, leaving exactly the number of threads designated in the bracketed stripe (see Figure 1)—that is, five threads on each end if you are making patterns A, B, or C (see Figure 2), and seven threads on each end if you are making pattern D. Lightly glue the short ends with all-purpose white glue and allow to dry.

Lay the five (or seven) unstitched threads at one end over those at the other end. Stitch through both layers of canvas to make an overlapping join (see Figure 3) and complete the stripe design.

Turn each napkin ring out and hem the excess canvas to the back of the stitching (see Figure 4). Turn right side out and line with the ribbon; hem the ends and blindstitch along the sides.

Decorating Bonus

Stitch napkin rings for children with lower-case letters, for their elders with capitals, especially if more than one name begins with the same initial.

Floral Ice Bucket

A panel of flowers and butterflies lies between two plastic cylinders to dress up an ice bucket (see "Sources").

To make the panel, use the following procedures, described in Section I:
- Preparing canvas
- Enlarging designs
- Transferring designs to canvas
- Stitching designs
- Blocking
- Protecting edges
- Joining
- Hemming
- Lining

Stitch

Basketweave

Canvas

No. 12 mono
Cut one piece 27 by 11 inches, and bind the edges with masking tape.

Yarn

You will need about 4 ounces of Persian wool.

Additional Materials

thin fabric for lining, ½ inch larger all around than the finished needlepoint

Enlarging and Transferring

Enlarge the design so that the width measures 22½ inches; the height will be about 6⅜ inches.

Center the enlarged design face up under the canvas and, using an indelible marker, trace it onto the canvas.

Special Tips for Work

Along the top and bottom of the canvas (the long edges), extend the design one additional row. On the sides of the canvas (the short edges), stop the design one thread short of the design outline (see Figure 1).

Finishing and Assembling

Block the needlepoint.

Sew a row of machine stitching on the excess canvas just outside the design outline.

Cut the excess canvas away on all four sides to within 1 inch of the needlepoint.

On the short edges, turn the excess canvas to the back, leaving just one row of canvas thread showing on each end (see Figure 43). Bring the ends together and baste the two threads together, matching rows for a butt join. Using appropriate color yarn, work over the basted row with a vertical outline stitch to complete the design (see Figure 45). Hem the excess canvas at the back of the

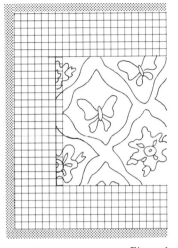

Figure 1

join to the inside of the needlepoint (see Figure 46).

Turn the excess canvas at the top edge to the inside and hem it to the back of the needlepoint. Repeat procedure for the bottom edge.

Fit the lining to the inside of the needlepoint, turning all hems under to make a neat finish. Blindstitch to the back of the needlepoint. Drop cylindrical panel into the ice bucket slot.

Decorating Bonus

Duplicate the flowers and butterflies on the diagonal patches individually for coasters; make them 4 inches square on interlocking canvas and finish the edges with the overcasting stitch.

1 space = 1 inch

Spanish-Motif Spray-Can Cover

Bathroom toiletries are often unsightly; conceal them attractively in a needlepoint disguise. This repeat design, derived from the Spanish artichoke motif, covers a medium-size can of hair spray; by extending the repeats at the top or sides, you can cover any cylindrical object from a short plump roll of toilet paper to a tall bottle of disinfectant. Don't worry about a custom fit; the covers should be roomy.

To make this particular cover, you will use the following basic procedures, which are described in detail in Section I:

- Preparing canvas
- Enlarging designs
- Transferring designs to canvas
- Stitching designs
- Blocking
- Protecting edges
- Joining
- Hemming
- Lining

Stitch

Basketweave

Canvas

No. 10 mono
Cut one piece 13 by 10 inches, and bind the edges with masking tape.

Yarn

You will need about 2 ounces of Persian wool.

Additional Materials

thin fabric for lining, 1 inch larger all around than the finished needlepoint

Enlarging and Transferring

Enlarge the design so that the width mea-

sures 9 inches; the height will be about 6⅜ inches.

Center the enlarged design face up under the canvas and, using an indelible marker, trace it onto the canvas.

Special Tips for Work

On the top and bottom (the long edges), extend the design one extra row. On the sides (the short edges), stop the design one thread short of the design outline (see Figure 1).

Finishing and Assembling

Block the needlepoint.

Sew a row of machine stitching on the excess canvas just outside the design outline.

Cut the excess canvas away on all four sides to within 1 inch of the needlepoint.

On the short edges, turn the excess canvas to the back, leaving just one row of canvas

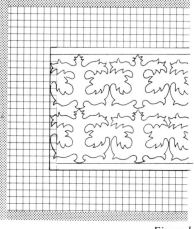

Figure 1

Figure 1

thread showing on each end (see Figure 43). Abut the ends together and baste the two threads together, matching rows for a butt join. Using appropriate color yarn, work over the basted row with a vertical outline stitch to complete the design (see Figure 45). Hem the excess canvas at the back of the join to the inside of the needlepoint (see Figure 46).

Turn the excess canvas at the top edge to the inside and hem it to the back of the needlepoint. Fit the lining to the inside of the needlepoint, turning all hems under to make a neat finish; blindstitch to the back of the needlepoint.

Decorating Bonus

Use the artichoke motif for coordinated bathroom accessories. For example, stitch one "artichoke" for a towel hanger; miter and hem the excess canvas, mount it on a wide ribbon, and hang it on a decorative hook.

Top your curtains with a simple valance made of one row of repeated motifs; miter and hem the excess canvas and then stretch it around two angle irons so that it hugs the curtains (see Figure 2).

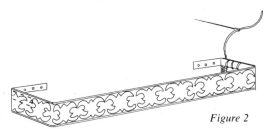

Figure 2

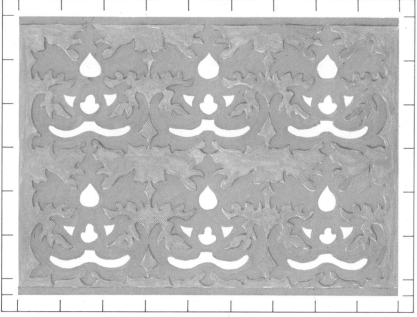

1 space = 1 inch

Chapter

8

Desk
Accessories

Sampler Typewriter Cover

The bold appeal of this typewriter cover derives from the use of the primary colors, including different shades of yellow, and the juxtaposition of the actual typewriter symbols with areas of colors and stitches. Only four different stitches appear, but they are used in different colors, different counts, and different directions to provide variety and texture and to contrast with blue denim case. The design offers a good opportunity to use up odd amounts of leftover yarn.

To make the cover, you will use the following basic procedures, which are described in detail in Section I:

- Preparing canvas
- Enlarging designs
- Transferring designs to canvas
- Stitching designs
- Blocking
- Protecting edges
- Lining
- Welting

Stitch

Basketweave behind all letters and numbers
Brick both horizontally and vertically
Gobelin over two, three, four, and five threads
Scotch in all its variations (see Figure 1)

Canvas

No. 12 mono
Cut one piece 22 by 24 inches, and bind the edges with masking tape.

Yarn

You will need about 7½ ounces of Persian wool.

Additional Materials

fabric for the sides, lining, welting, and binding, about ¾ yard and 45 inches wide (see

Figure 2 for cutting plan)
lining, ½ inch larger all around than the finished needlepoint
2 strips of welting, each 22 inches long
bias binding, 1½ inches wide and 66 inches long

Enlarging and Transferring

Enlarge the design so that the length measures 21 inches; it will be about 18 inches at its widest point.

Center the enlarged design face up under the canvas and, using an indelible marker, trace it onto the canvas. Work the letters and numbers from the graphs on pages 184–186.

Special Tips for Work

Around all four edges, extend the design two extra rows to provide for a seam allowance.

Finishing and Assembling

Block the needlepoint.
Sew a row of machine stitching on the

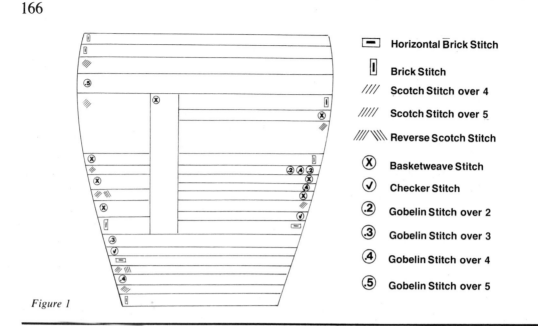

Figure 1

⊟	**Horizontal Brick Stitch**
▯	**Brick Stitch**
////	**Scotch Stitch over 4**
////	**Scotch Stitch over 5**
////\\\\	**Reverse Scotch Stitch**
Ⓧ	**Basketweave Stitch**
Ⓥ	**Checker Stitch**
②	**Gobelin Stitch over 2**
③	**Gobelin Stitch over 3**
④	**Gobelin Stitch over 4**
⑤	**Gobelin Stitch over 5**

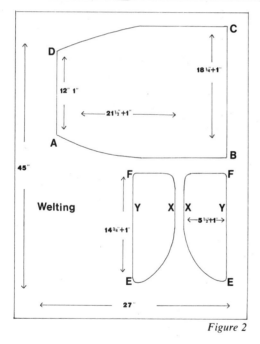

Figure 2

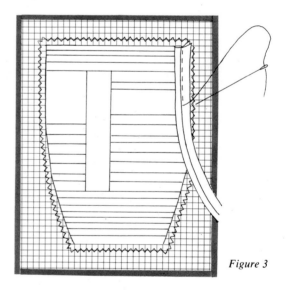

allowance. Baste and then sew them together on top of the welting seam (see Figure 3). Repeat for the opposite side.

Figure 3

excess canvas just outside the needlepoint.

Lay the needlepoint face up. Place one length of welting over one long side so that its unfinished edge is pointed out toward the taped canvas edge and the seam of the welting is directly over the needlepoint seam

Lay the left side piece face down on the left welting, matching its long curved edge (see EXF in Figure 2) to the welted side of the needlepoint. Baste and then sew them together on the seam allowance (see Figure

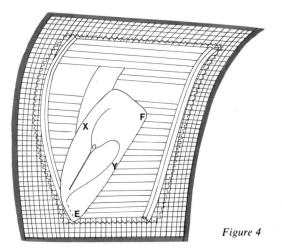

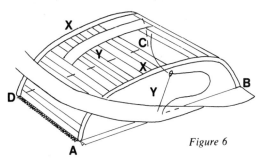

Place the binding all along the bottom edge of the typewriter cover (see AYB, BC, CYD, and DA in Figure 2), right sides together, and sew on top of the seam allowances. Turn the binding under and blindstitch to the inside (see Figure 6).

Figure 4

Figure 6

4). Repeat for opposite side using right side piece.

Around all four sides, trim the excess canvas and fabric to within ½ inch of the needlepoint.

Pin the lining to the needlepoint, wrong sides together. On each long edge, turn the lining under ½ inch and blindstitch it to the back of the needlepoint (see Figure 5). Leave the top and bottom edges unstitched.

Adjusting the Design Area

This particular cover fits a portable electric typewriter; its dimensions can be altered by extending or curtailing the pattern at the sides of the top and bottom strips (see Figure 7). Be sure to adjust the side pieces, welting, and binding as well.

Decorating Bonus

Substitute a monogram or company logotype for the name; use the checkerboard pattern in a desk set (see page 171).

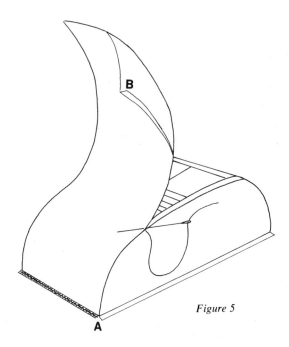

Figure 5

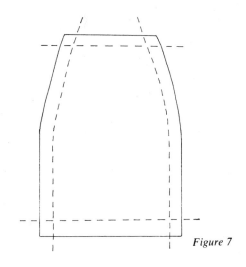

Figure 7

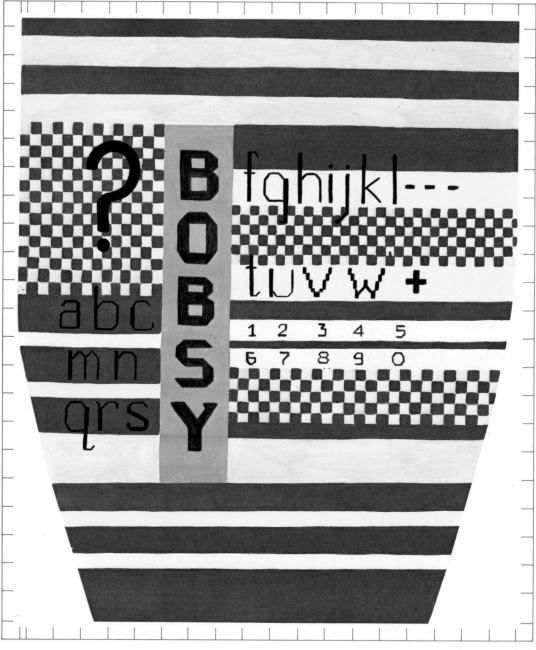

1 space = 1 inch

Mosaic-Style Letter-Tray Cover

Hide your desk top clutter in a letter tray handsomely covered with needlepoint. This particular geometric design, derived from a tile floor in the Basilica of St. Mark, Venice, fits an outsize plastic tray (see "Sources"), but could easily be adapted for regulation letter- or legal-size trays sold in stationery stores.

To make the cover, you will use the following basic procedures, which are described in detail in Section I:

- Preparing canvas
- Transferring designs to canvas
- Stitching designs
- Blocking
- Protecting edges
- Mitering corners
- Lining

Stitch

Basketweave

Canvas

No. 10 mono

Cut one piece 16 by 18 inches, and bind the edges with masking tape.

Yarn

You will need about 5 ounces of Persian wool.

Additional Materials

stiff cardboard, 11½ by 13⅓ inches
white porcelain pull or decorative knob with
a short matching screw or bolt
felt for lining

Enlarging and Transferring

Work the design in Figure 1 to measure 12 by 14 inches, starting at the center with a terra-cotta diamond and working out. You

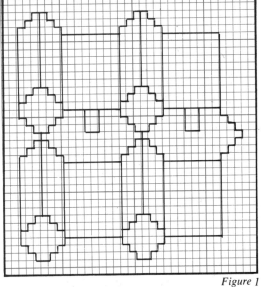

Figure 1

can establish the pattern easily by stitching the gray rectangles first, followed by the terra-cotta diamonds, the black and beige forms, and lastly the white areas.

Finishing and Assembling

Block the needlepoint.

Sew a row of machine stitching on the excess canvas just outside the needlepoint.

Cut the excess canvas away on all four sides to within 1½ inches of the needlepoint, and cut the corners diagonally to within 1 inch of the stitching.

Punch a small hole the diameter of the screw through the center of the cardboard. Lay the needlepoint face down and center the cardboard over it. Temporarily anchor the needlepoint to the edge of the cardboard with stick pins, making sure that the rows of stitching are straight (see Figure 2).

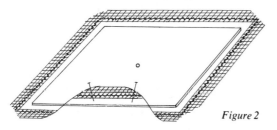

Figure 2

With all-purpose white resin glue, stick opposite sides of the canvas to the cardboard, starting in the center of the sides and working to within 2 inches of each corner. Cover the glued area with waxed paper and weight with a heavy book until glue has dried. Miter each corner and glue all edges to the cardboard (see Figure 3). Weight down as above and let glue dry.

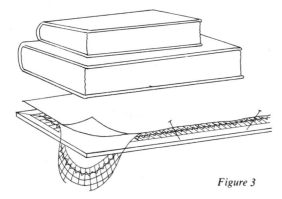

Figure 3

Through the hole in the cardboard, insert the screw or bolt from the underside, poking it carefully between the needlepoint stitches so that it does not split the yarn (see Figure

4). Attach the decorative pull; you may have to shorten the screw for a proper fit.

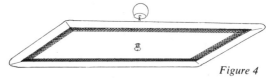

Figure 4

Cut felt lining to size and glue to the back, covering the screwhead and the unstitched canvas (see Figure 5).

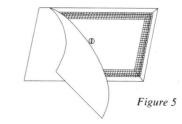

Figure 5

Adjusting the Design Area

To make a tray cover of different size, cut the cardboard backing at least ¼ inch smaller than the interior dimensions of your letter tray and then stitch the required design area plus two rows all around for finishing. Mount as described above.

Decorating Bonus

The class geometric design and neutral color scheme make this cover appropriate in many out-boxes—an elegant executive oiled-wood letter tray, a modest gray metal tray, a dressier wicker version. Small trays can be placed in a home entrance hall for mail; larger sizes in workrooms to catch extra clutter.

Checkered Desk Blotter

Desk-top organizers in handsome checks will dress up any style of desk. Just vary the color of the checks to suit executive or student. The desk pad is clear acrylic (see "Sources") to cradle blotter and decorative needlepoint panels. Instructions for the pencil holder are on page 173.

To make the desk blotter, you will use the following basic procedures, which are described in detail in Section I:
- Preparing canvas
- Stitching designs
- Joining
- Blocking

Stitch

Basketweave

Overcasting on edges

Canvas

No. 12 interlocking

Cut two pieces, each measuring 8 by 21 inches, and bind the cut edges with masking tape.

Yarn

You will need about 3½ ounces of Persian wool.

Additional Materials

acrylic desk pad, 24 by 16 inches overall, including 4-inch-wide panels at each side

172

Enlarging and Transferring

Each colored box is five stitches square; the checkered pattern is established by alternating colors.

Start at the top right corner of the canvas (at the bottom left corner if you are left-handed), 2 inches in from each edge. Work the checkered pattern until your needlepoint is nine boxes wide and forty boxes high. However, along all four edges, stop the pattern one row short—that is, the boxes at the top and bottom will be five stitches wide but only four stitches high and the boxes at the sides will be four stitches wide and five stitches high (see Figure 1).

Finishing and Assembling

Block the needlepoint.

Along all four edges, carefully cut the canvas one row outside the existing needle-point, leaving one thread all around. Finish the edges with an overcasting stitch (see Figure 29). As you overcast along the checkered edges, work with two threaded needles and change yarn color to match the alternating boxes, carrying the unused thread under the overcast edge.

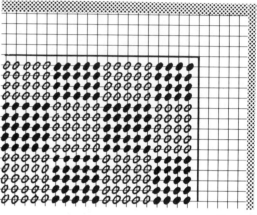

Figure 1

Checkered Pencil Holder

The pencil holder shown on page 171 is really an orange juice can in disguise.

To make the pencil holder, you will use the following basic procedures, which are described in detail in Section I:

- Preparing canvas
- Stitching designs
- Joining
- Blocking

Stitch

Basketweave
Overcasting on edges

Canvas

No. 12 interlocking

Cut one piece 9 by 13 inches, and bind the edges with masking tape.

Yarn

You will need about 1½ ounces of Persian wool.

Additional Materials

juice can, large size (12-ounce)
fabric tape, to match one of the colors, 1½ inches wide and 9 inches long

Enlarging and Transferring

Each colored box is five stitches square; the checkered pattern is established by alternating colors.

Start at the top right corner of the canvas (at the bottom left corner if you are left-handed), 2 inches in from each edge. Work the checkered pattern until your needlepoint is twenty-one boxes wide and twelve boxes high. However, along the top and bottom edges (the long sides), stop the pattern one row short—that is, all the boxes along the top and bottom will be five stitches wide but

only four stitches high (see Figure 1).

Finishing and Assembling

Block the needlepoint.

On each short end, cut the excess canvas,

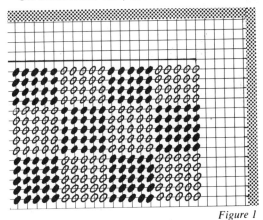

Figure 1

leaving exactly five threads on each. Lightly glue the cut ends with all-purpose white resin glue and let dry.

Lay the five unstitched threads at one end over those at the other end. Stitch through both layers of canvas to make an overlapping join, continuing in the checkered pattern. Remember that the boxes at the top and bottom will only be four rows high (see Figure 2).

Along the top and bottom edges, carefully cut the canvas one row outside the existing needlepoint, leaving one thread (see Figure 3). Finish the top and bottom edges with an overcasting stitch in yarn to match (see Figure 4). As you come to the overlapping join, finish it in the same way.

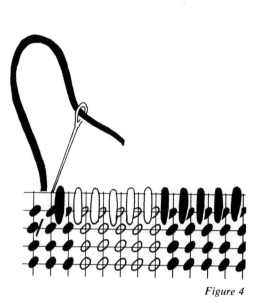

Figure 4

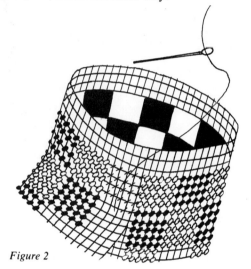

Figure 2

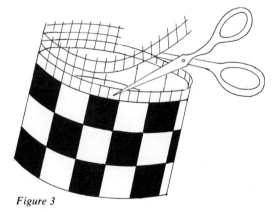

Figure 3

Finish the top edge of the juice can as follows: Cut the fabric tape, if necessary, to fit the circumference. Place the tape so that half its width encircles the top of the can; the other half will extend over the top edge (see Figure 5). Snip the extended part of the tape

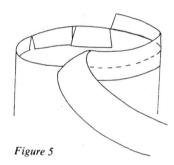

Figure 5

every inch or so. Fold these tabs back and glue them to the inside of the can, where they will partially overlap each other (see Figure 5). Line the inside of the can with self-adhesive decorative paper if desired.

Pull the finished needlepoint cylinder over the orange juice can. If you find that it fits too loosely, pad with a thin underlayer of cotton batting.

Decorating Bonus

Personalize one or both desk items with initials from pages 184 and 185.

Botanical-Print Bookends

Embrace a group of books on top of your desk with this pair of flower-bedecked bookends. The covers slip over standard metal bookends available at stationery stores.

To make the botanical-print bookend covers, you will use the following procedures, which are described in detail in Section I:

- Preparing canvas
- Enlarging designs
- Transferring designs to canvas
- Stitching designs
- Blocking
- Protecting edges
- Lining
- Hemming

Stitch

Basketweave

Canvas

No. 12 mono

Cut two pieces of canvas, each measuring 8 by 9 inches, and bind the cut edges with masking tape.

Yarn

For the pair, you will need almost 2 ounces of Persian wool; 1 ounce of it will be used for the background.

Additional Materials

2 pieces of fabric for lining

Enlarging and Transferring

Enlarge each design so that its width measures 4¾ inches; the height will be about 5⅜ inches.

Center each enlarged design face up under the canvas and, using an indelible marker, trace it onto the canvas.

Special Tips for Work

Around all edges, extend the design two extra rows.

Finishing and Assembling

Block the pieces of needlepoint.

Sew a row of machine stitching on the excess canvas just ouside the needlepoint on each piece.

Lay each piece of needlepoint face down on its lining. Along the top and both sides, baste and then sew a seam just inside the seam allowance; gently round off the corners (see Figure 1).

Cut excess canvas and lining away on all sides to within 1 inch of needlepoint; cut two top corners diagonally.

Figure 1

Figure 2

Turn right side out and, at the bottom, hem both the lining and the unstitched canvas separately (see Figure 2).

Decorating Bonus

Center a handsome monogram for a bibliophile who treasures his books.

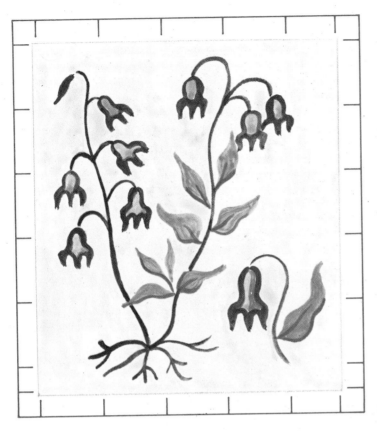

1 space = 1 inch

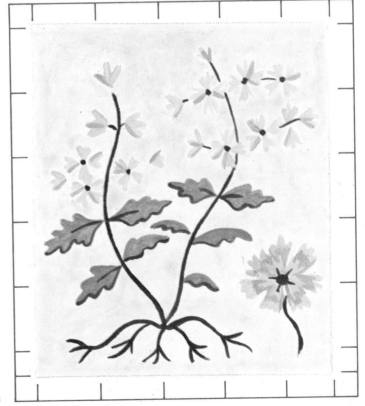

1 space = 1 inch

Swatchbook of Needlepoint Designs

This swatchbook is really a collection of ready-to-upholster needlepoint fabrics, from charming chintzes to bold geometrics.

Each of the allover design swatches can be used with any of the projects in Section II; together they multiply your opportunities for decorating with needlepoint. Enlarge them, repeat them, or extend them, and then substitute any for the project designs.

If the colors of the swatches don't fit your home exactly, replace them with colors that do. The swatchbook is presented so that you can custom-stitch prints that will delight your eye and enhance your home. Also included in this section are an upper-case and lowercase alphabet plus a set of numbers to further extend your needlepoint possibilities.

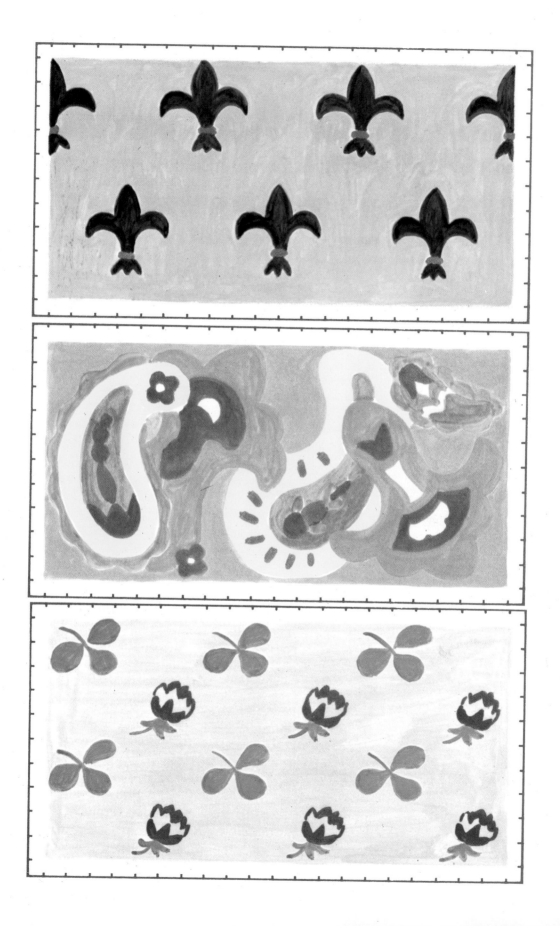

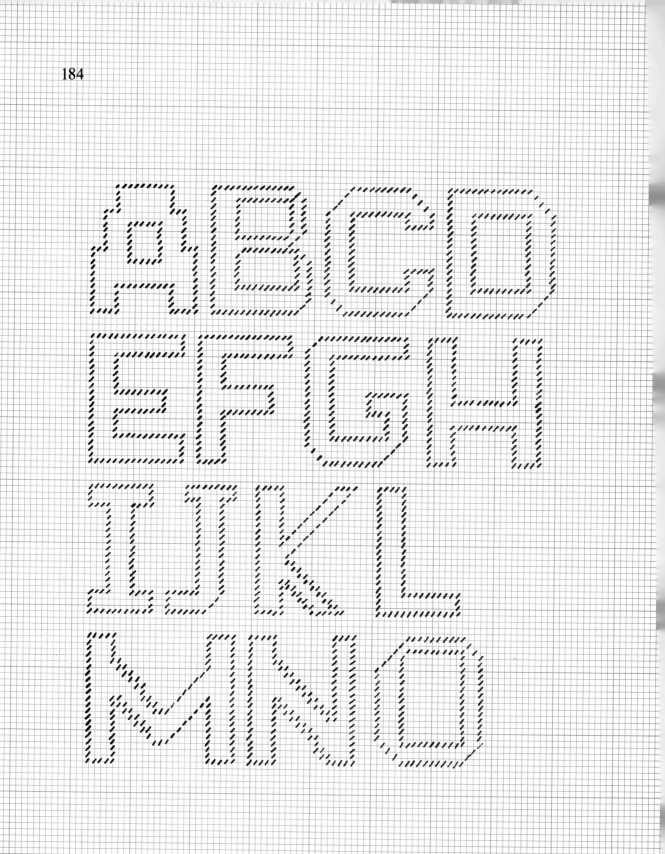

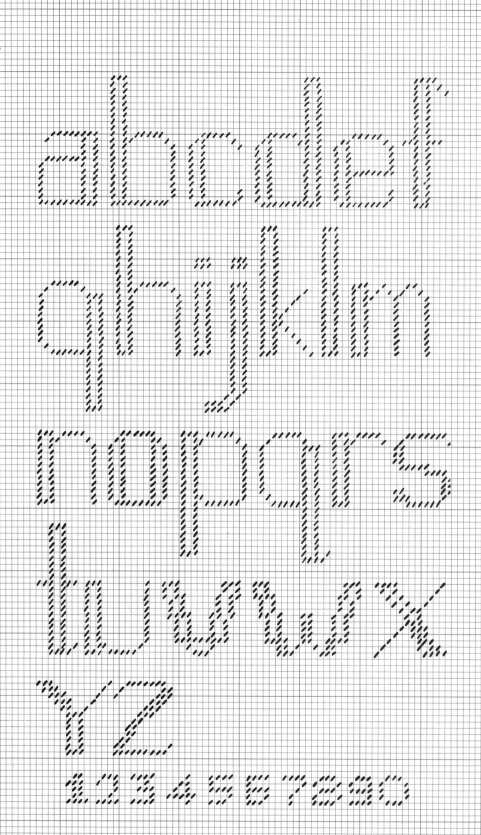

Material Source List

Some of the needlepoint projects in this book require special materials. These are listed below, along with a mail order source for each:

backgammon table—Canal Street Plastics, 115 Cedar St., New Rochelle, N.Y. 10801

desk pad—Toni Totes of Vermont, Inc., S. Londonderry, Vt. 05155

footstool—Aa Creative Design, Woodlands Rd., Harrison, N.Y. 10528

ice bucket—Hilde's Knit Shop, 305 White Plains Post Rd., Eastchester, N.Y. 10709

lamp base—Hilde's Knit Shop, 305 White Plains Post Rd., Eastchester, N.Y. 10709

letter tray—Aa Creative Design, Woodlands Rd., Harrison, N.Y. 10528

picture frame—Canal Street Plastics, 115 Cedar St., New Rochelle, N.Y. 10801

prefinished pillow—Toni Totes of Vermont, Inc., S. Londonderry, Vt. 05155

serving tray—Hilde's Knit Shop, 305 White Plains Post Rd., Eastchester, N.Y. 10709

A large number of shops carry needlepoint supplies. Look for those most convenient to you in the classified pages of your telephone book. They are usually listed under "Art Needlework." The following is an alphabetical list of retail sources by state:

The Needleworks, 2906 Linden Ave., Birmingham, Ala. 35209

The Needlepoint Nook, 5037 N. Seventh Ave., Phoenix, Ariz. 85013

The Nimble Thimble, P.O. Box 713, Aptos, Calif. 95003

Petit Point Junction, 373 N. Robertson Blvd., Los Angeles, Calif. 90048

Lazy Daisy Needlecraft Shop, 602 E. Walnut St., Pasadena, Calif. 91101

The Knittery, 2040 Union St., San Francisco, Calif. 94123

Nimble Needle, 2645 San Diego Ave., San Diego, Calif. 92110

The Needlecraft Shop, 4501 Van Nuys Blvd., Sherman Oaks, Calif. 91403

The Yarn Garden, Williams Village Shopping Center, 651 30th St., Boulder, Colo. 80302

Golden Needle, 2356 E. Third Ave., Denver, Colo. 80206

The Knitting Needle, 2128 So. Albion St., Denver, Colo. 80222

The Point, 755 So. Colorado Blvd., Denver, Colo. 80222

Valley Handicrafters, Avon, Conn. 06001

The Designing Woman, Lakeville, Conn. 06039

The Daisy, 998 Farmington Ave., W. Hartford, Conn. 06107

Colonial Yarn Shop, Inc., 3830 Kennett Pike, Wilmington, Del. 19807

The Elegant Needle, 5430 MacArthur Blvd. N.W., Washington, D.C. 20016

Needlepoint Design by Lou Gartner, 312 Worth Ave., Palm Beach, Fla. 33480

Needle Nook, 6488 Central Ave., St. Petersburg, Fla. 33707

Papillon, Gates Plaza, 375 Pharr Rd. N.E., Atlanta, Ga. 30305

Felker Art Needlework, Inc., 640 Valleybrook Road, Decatur, Ga. 30033

Needlepoint Works, Inc., 1660 N. La Salle St., Chicago, Ill. 60614

Nimble Needles, 340 W. Armitage Ave., Chicago, Ill. 60614

Nina Needlepoint, 120 E. Delaware Place, Chicago, Ill. 60611

Wild & Woolly, Inc., 5210 S. Harper Ave., Chicago, Ill. 60615

Flying Colors, 20 W. Hinsdale Ave., Hinsdale, Ill. 60521

Magic Needle, 44 Green Bay Road, Winnetka, Ill. 60093

Christian Decker Shop, Old Court House, Room 113, Evansville, Ind. 47708

Constance Ann's Needlepoint, 6502 E. Westfield Blvd., Indianapolis, Ind. 46220

Craft Kaleidoscope, 6412 Ferfeson St., Indianapolis, Ind. 46220

Town Stitchery, 6516 Cornell Ave., Indianapolis, Ind. 46220

Mrs. Madness, 1835 Second Ave. S.E., Cedar Rapids, Iowa 52403

The Little Needlepoint Shop, 223 Forest Rd., Davenport, Iowa 52803

Creative Corner, Inc., 332 Fifth St., West Des Moines, Iowa 50265

Golden Thimble, Inc., 515 Maple St., West Des Moines, Iowa 50265

Needle Nook, 7135 W. 80 St., Kansas City, Kans.

The Crewel Cupboard, 15 E. Eighth St., Lawrence, Kan. 66044

In Stitches, 3901 Prairie La. Prairie Village, Kans. 66208

Duquesa, 1901 Brookwood Rd., Shawnee Mission, Kan. 66208

Needlepoint by Meg, 133 Woodlawn Ct. Wichita, Kans. 67218

Needlepoint, Inc., 2401 Magazine St., New Orleans, La. 70130

Needle Works, Ltd., 4041 Tulane Ave., New Orleans, La. 70119

The Quarter Stitch, 532 St. Peter St., New Orleans, La. 70116

Where It's At, 2 Winthrop St., Augusta, Maine 04330

Needle Arts, Inc., 28 Washington St., Camden, Maine 04843

The Blunt Needle, 720 Deepdene Rd., Baltimore, Md. 20210

Needlecraft Shop, Yorktown Plaza Shopping Center, Baltimore, Md. 21030

Craft Kit & Caboodle, 10400 Old Georgetown Rd., Bethesda, Md. 20314

The Needlecraft Center, 1079 Rockville Pike, Rockville, Md. 20852

Nimble Fingers, Inc., 37 Newbury St., Boston, Mass. 02116

Needlecraft House, West Townsend, Mass. 01474

Nantucket Needleworks, 11 South Water St., Nantucket Island, Mass. 02554

The Stitchery, 204 Worcester Tpke., Wellesley, Mass. 02181

Needlepoint a la Carte, 325 S. Woodward, Birmingham, Mich. 48011

Needle Arts, Inc., 2211 Monroe St., Dearborn, Mich. 48124

Peacock Alley, 650 Croswell S.E., Grand Rapids, Mich. 49506

Crewel Studio, 19587 Mack Ave., Grosse Pointe, Mich. 48236

The Needling Woman, 14421 Oak Park Rd., Oak Park, Mich. 48237

The Jeweled Needle, 1009 Nicollet Ave., Minneapolis, Minn. 55403

Needlework Unlimited, Inc., 5028 France Ave. S., Minneapolis, Minn. 55410

The Picket Fence, Inc., 3924 Upton Ave. S. Minneapolis, Minn. 55410

Stitch Niche, 2866 Hennepin Ave. S. Minneapolis, Minn. 55408

The Needle Nest, 729 E. Lake St., Wayzata, Minn. 55391

The Studio, 316 W. 63 St., Kansas City, Mo. 64113

Kirck Kits, 31 N. Brentwood Blvd., St. Louis, Mo. 63105

Needlepoint, Etc., 9841 Clayton Rd., St. Louis, Mo. 63124

Sign of the Arrow, 8740 Clayton Rd., St. Louis, Mo. 63124

Jo's Stitchery, 510 S. Elm, North Platte, Neb. 69101

Needlepoint Studio, 8707 Shamrock Road, Omaha, Neb. 68114

Stitch Witchery, Rte. 10, P.O. Box N, Denville, N.J. 07834

L'Image, 100 Main St., Fort Lee, N.J. 07024

The Knitting Needle, Armonk, N.Y. 10504

T. E. Goelger, Box 126, Blauvelt, N.Y. 10913

Niddy Noddy, 416 Albany Post Rd., Croton-on-Hudson, N.Y. 10520

Hilde's Knit Shop, 305 White Plains Post Rd., Eastchester, N.Y. 10709

Creative Canvas, Inc., 113 Main St., Irvington, N.Y. 10533

Katharine Knox, 445 Plandome Rd., Manhasset, N.Y. 11030

Boutique Margot, 26 W. 54 St., New York, N.Y. 10019

Alice Maynard, 724 Fifth Ave., New York, N.Y. 10022

Mazaltov's, Inc., 758 Madison Ave., New York, N.Y. 10021

Selma's Art Needlework, 1645 Second Ave., New York, N.Y. 10028

Black Sheep, 44 Purchase St., Rye, N.Y. 10580

The Needleworks, 90 E. Post Rd., White Plains, N.Y. 10606

Needlepoint Only, 12801 Larchmere Blvd., Cleveland, Ohio 44120

Contemporary Stitchery, 2905 N. High St., Columbus, Ohio 43202

Needlepoint Designs, 5210 E. Main St., Columbus, Ohio 43213

Elizabeth Lamprey Studio, 5940 S. Lewis Ave., Tulsa, Okla. 74105

Creative Hands, 515 S.W. Broadway, Portland, Ore. 97205

Flying Colours, 1016 S.W. Morrison, Portland, Ore. 97205

Needlepoint Corner, 8121 Old York Rd., Elkins Park, Pa. 19117

The Needlepoint Garden, 7518 Haverford Ave., Philadelphia, Pa. 19151

The Needle's Eye, 1724 Sansom St., Philadelphia, Pa. 19103

The Thread Shed, Inc., 307 Freeport Rd., Pittsburgh, Pa. 15212

Needlepointer, 793 Hope St., Providence, R.I. 02906

Indie, 618 S. Semmes, Memphis, Tenn. 38111

Canvas Patch Originals, P.O. Box 3072, Oak Ridge, Tenn. 37830

Needle Art Boutique, 2800 Routh St., Dallas, Tex. 75201

Needlework Patio, 6925 Snider Plaza, Dallas, Tex. 75205

The Silver Needle, Inc., 6100 Camp Bowie Blvd., Fort Worth, Tex. 76116

Virginia Maxwell Custom Needlework Studio, 3404 Kirby Dr., Houston, Tex. 77006

The Knit Shop, 3516 S. Shepherd Dr., Houston, Tex. 77006

Knit-Wits, 1379 E. #205 St. S., Salt Lake City, Utah 84106

Needlecraft Ltd., 1615 Foothill Dr., Salt Lake City, Utah 84108

Yarn Bazaar, 421 S. Washington St., Alexandria, Va. 22314

Yarns Etcetera, 215 King St., Alexandria, Va. 22314

The Woolly Bear, Ballard Rd., Charlottesville, Va. 22901

Petite Point Junction, 13860 Midlothian Tpke., Midlothian, Va. 23113

Needlework Nook, 431 Forest Ave., Richmond, Va. 23223

Corner Stitch, Ltd., 25th and Pacific Ave., Virginia Beach, Va. 23451

The Needlepoint Studio, 6501 20th Ave. N.E., Seattle, Wash. 98115

The Needle Works, 4518 39th Pl. N.E., Seattle, Wash. 98105

The Needleworks, 116 W. Silver Spring Dr., Milwaukee, Wis. 53217

Ruhama's Yarn and Fabrics, 420 Silver Spring Dr., Milwaukee, Wis. 53217

Frederick Herrschner Co., Hoover Rd., Stevens Point, Wis. 54481

The following is a list of Canadian sources:
Brickpoint Studios, 2195 Crescent St., Montreal, Que.

Jeannette's Needlecraft Shoppe, 5322 Queen Mary, Montreal, Que.

In Stitches Gallery, 102 Yorkville St., Toronto, Ont.

Martha Borbas Needlepoint Gallery, 1613 Bayview Ave., Toronto, Ont.

The Added Touch, 3026 Granville St., Vancouver, B.C.

Woolcraft (B.C.) Ltd., 512 W. Hastings St., Vancouver, B.C.

Needleworks, 156 Spence St., Winnipeg, Man.

Lucite accessories for needlepoint, such as desk pads, napkin holders, desk organizers, bookends, parson's tables, and pencil holders, can be ordered through Toni Totes of Vermont, Inc., South Londonderry, Vt. 05155

Index